Titani

(

One Liners

By

Gary Rowley

All aboard, all aboard!

Get your tickets, if you dare, for a hysterical voyage of mirth and merriment aboard the *Titanic Book of One Liners*, awash with a calamitous cargo of hundreds of rib-tickling original jokes and puns.

Guaranteed to go down a treat, you'll discover oceans of good, clean fun, ammunition aplenty to deliver an endless barrage of hilarious broadsides upon unsuspecting family and friends.

Victims will be at sea, steaming for port, desperately trying to fathom the source of the onslaught, blissfully unaware it's merely the calm before the storm. And all you'll need to do to continue the punishment is sit back, relax, and slowly turn the page...

Thar she blows, shipmates – bon voyage!!!

Dedicated to joke lovers everywhere... salute!

I went to see a comedian that told a hundred jokes in a row, all about the Titanic. Him and his one liners...

Straight after, it was a comedian called Humpty Dumpty. Honestly, he was so off the wall.

Then it was this geezer who only knew jokes about Typhoo and PG Tips. Nah, I thought: not my cup of tea.

I was back again next night for a comedian who spent the entire gig flat on his back. I said, I thought this was meant to be stand up...?

And then there was the geezer who insisted on switching the lights out before he came on stage. You can't beat a bit of dark humour...

He was definitely a step up in class from the wally whose entire act was filled with Smurf jokes. He was far too blue for my liking.

As for the comedian who told towel jokes all night, well...dry sense of humour didn't come into it.

Anyway, I've got a couple of jokes of my own I think you might like. If I tell you the one about butter, will you promise not to spread it?

Or I could tell you another about a brick wall. Trouble is, I don't think you'd ever get over it.

Here's one, then: how about you take your pick from hundreds of original jokes, puns and one liners to follow? Just like the Titanic, I guarantee they'll go down a treat...

*   *   *

I was involved in a prang with an Elvis impersonator. I was alright, like, but he was all shook up...

I phoned the police after a lorry shed its load of cutlery outside our house. Asked where exactly, I said, turn left at the fork in the road...

3

It's just been on the news that a trio of cliff walkers perished overnight. Imagine that, I thought: three people and all with the same name as well.

There was this bloke, running around, screaming his ear had been chopped off. Is that it? I asked, pointing at the floor. No, he replied, mine had a pencil on it.

Traffic chaos ensued earlier when a lorry load of Vick nasal spray collided with a lorry load of Sudafed tablets. Thankfully, congestion is now starting to ease.

In a separate incident, a short-tongued lorry driver was arrested on suspicion of dangerous driving after spilling his load of men's apparel across three lanes of busy motorway. The road remains clothed until further notice…

This bloke asked if I watched last night's documentary about the 1929 Wall Street Crash. Wow, I thought: it must have been some accident if they're still talking about it 88 years later!

So I said, my cash for crush compensation didn't last long. He said, don't you mean cash for crash? I said, no, crush: I spent every penny on dilute orange.

Did you hear about the steam engine fanatic who was run over by the Flying Scotsman? He was dead chuffed.

I had a bad accident at the saw mill. My other half says we should sue for compensation.

Anyone seen my flat mate? Yup, that's him: the one who was run over by a steamroller.

I rang this personal injury specialist. I said, how much to break my boss's legs for him…?

*   *   *

I love living in our house. It's right up my street.

People think I'm nuts for buying a house on a street with no name. I don't know why: it's not something I can't address later.

My new pen pal lives in an apartment at the top of the Empire State Building. How about that for friends in high places?

I come from a broken home. All the windows are smashed, the front door's been ripped off, and there's no gas or electricity…

I've just had my house draught-proofed. This company came round, spent ten minutes shivering, then gave me written proof: I *definitely* have a draught.

I was over the moon when my bid for a flat was accepted. I wasn't quite so cock-a-hoop when I found out I'd paid a hundred grand for a tyre with a hole in it.

Every time there's a row in our house, my mother sides with my little brother, Gabriel. Honestly, she thinks he's a right little angel.

I asked this bloke what his favourite Elvis song was. In the ghetto, came the reply. I said, don't be so rude: I live in a three-bedroomed semi near the park.

I bumped into this ex-army officer, roughing it in the high street toilets. Whey hey, I thought: it's a loo-tenant.

New Orleans: rumour has it there's a house there…

* * *

I love my job at the electric kettle factory. In actual fact, I'm in my element.

I've still no idea where I put the colander. Honestly, I've got a mind like a blooming sieve.

I opened the cupboard and there was this tin of soup, trembling like a leaf. I said, what are you, chicken…?

Last night's housewarming party certainly lived up to its billing: the flipping kitchen caught fire.

Whenever we go on holiday, the wife insists upon taking everything but the kitchen sink. Last year, she even tried packing Encyclopaedia Britannica. That was when I put my foot down. Right, I said, the book stops here...

First night in the new gaff, a troop of ceremonial soldiers went galloping through the living room and began forming up in the kitchen. Whey hey, I thought: it's the household cavalry.

There's a new Mel Gibson film coming out about a mass murderer that does for his victims with a cheese toastie machine. Tefal Weapon is due for release next week.

Egg and a sausage in a frying pan. Egg says: Warm in here, innit? Sausage says: I didn't know eggs could talk!

That job in the kitchen worktop factory, it looks like our kid's got it...touch Formica.

What's red and white and sits in a kitchen? A fridge with a Manchester United shirt on.

*   *   *

This bloke stopped me and asked I'd seen his back garden anywhere. I said, have you lost the plot...?

Setting up a leaf removal service was the best thing I ever did. Honestly, I'm absolutely raking it in.

I was out raking the lawn when Mick Jagger walked past. I said, fancy giving us a hand, Mick? He said, haven't you heard, mister? A Rolling Stone gathers no moss.

I was having a right old ding-dong with the next door neighbour when this wasp landed on his nose. I didn't let it sting him. I made sure I got it first with my shovel.

Our kid went out with a strimmer under one arm and a Flymo under the other. He said, don't worry, I'll be back in a mow...

Every time the phone rings, it's this voice saying there's someone planting big trees at the bottom of my garden. I'm sick of all these blooming oaks calls...

When my tree felling business hit hard times, I sacked the manager then ordered an immediate root and branch review...

Me and the bloke who invented reclining chairs: we don't half go back a long way.

I poured a bottle of gin on the front lawn. Ten minutes later, it was half cut.

I had a crack at landscape gardening. But I can't say I pulled any trees up.

I'm saving up for a new privet. I keep the cash in my hedge fund.

*   *   *

I woke to find the bedroom filled with eggs. Oh no, I thought: I've overlaid again...

Next night, I forgot to turn the landing light off. When I got up, there was a jumbo jet parked outside the bathroom door.

There was this bloke in pyjamas, snoring his head off, while running the 100 metres in 9.7 seconds. I thought, he's fast asleep...

I went to bed Sunday night and woke next morning to find myself surrounded by dozens of cartoon bears, singing The Bare Necessities. It was a bad case of Monday morning Baloo's.

Someone said there was a job going at Kwik Fit. Tyres and exhausts, the advert said. I'll bet it does, I thought, eyeing up a bed tester's vacancy instead...

This bloke from the Inland Revenue came round and asked if he could scatter small, flat-headed nails over my upstairs carpets. I soon told him where to go with his blooming bedroom tacks.

So I said, why is the laptop wrapped up in bed with a hot water bottle...? *Please* tell me it's not frozen again!

First night in the new house and I couldn't get to sleep for this infernal ticking noise. I think it must have been the neighbourhood watch.

When Rooney missed a penalty, I ran on the pitch, broke his legs, then pushed the goalposts over. Mum sent me straight to bed and put my Subbuteo back in the cupboard.

I looked out of the window and there was this bloke, stealing my gates. I didn't say anything, like; I was scared he might have taken a fence.

This bloke offered to sell me a bed for a tenner. I told him I was definitely interested...but I'd prefer to sleep on it first.

*   *   *

Norman next door absolutely despises our William. Talk about Billy Norm hates...

A baby goat's moved in two doors down. It's the new kid on the block...

When the woman in the house across ran out of multi-surface cleaner, I said she could have mine. I meant it as well: I gave her my Pledge.

The long distance lorry driver that's moved in next door bitterly regrets flogging his sat nav. He says he's lost without it...

The new couple opposite: they're rugby league mad, eat black pudding and tripe, and speak with thick east Yorkshire accents. Just my luck, I thought: neighbours from Hull.

So I said, I've just heard the girl next door has signed a lucrative Hollywood film contract. He said, Warner Brothers? I said, course I did: I warned her sisters as well, plus everyone else in the street.

I fell out with the lumberjack upstairs. We were at loggerheads for weeks.

I fell out with the axe murderer below as well. Not for long, though: we soon buried the hatchet.

By coincidence, my sister married an axe murderer. Apparently this axe upset him one day, so he grabbed it by the handle and threw it off the edge of a cliff.

The bloke across the road, the one who collects waterproof, padded jackets. What an anorak!

* * *

I found a hedgehog in my pint. I thought, this has been spiked.

Did you know one in 50 people in the UK are borderline alcoholic? Staggering.

I got drunk at the pub. Two days later, I still haven't worked out whose belly I'm in.

Just before the pub shut, I ordered Thai spring rolls, prosciutto melon and a cheese board. It was last hors d'oeuvres.

I went down the pub and got poked in the eye by an antler. Blooming stag party!

The night after, I went home early on account of a raucous Hen party. All that clucking was driving me bonkers.

I've joined this club where no one knows anyone's name and all we do is go out and get hammered every day. If you need us, you'll find us in the phone book under alcoholics anonymous...

So I said, how about we crack open a couple of beers then stick some classic sci-fi on? He said, Intersteller? I said, I am, like; but I'd prefer a drop of your dad's home brew if there's any going spare.

I said, doctor, doctor, I keep thinking I'm a pint of lager. He said, please don't be bitter...

Umpteen pieces of string and twine went on a night out and everyone got a round in. Except for the tight rope, of course.

There was this bloke, having a pint on the pub roof. I think he quite got it when the landlord called drinks on the house.

Did you hear about the landlord who caught his barmaid, siphoning off ale? He didn't half let her have it...both empty barrels.

*   *   *

In the 2017 Cumbrian sheep dog trials, how many animals were found guilty?

I said, what's the name of the ship on the film, Mutiny on the Bounty? He said, is it the Mayflower?

No way on earth was I entering the blooming general knowledge quiz. You could write on the back a postage stamp what I know about military top brass.

So I said, who had a number one hit with Tiger Feet? Mud! came the reply. I said, that's right, that's right, that's right, that's right...

I was doing brilliant in the pub quiz until question 15: who had a hit with The Very Best of Rod Stewart? How was I supposed to know? I wasn't born until 1999.

As for question 23, I just ignored it: name the perpetrators of the Great Train Robbery. I knew the answer, naturally: I'm just not a grass, that's all.

Quizmaster: Name a French City famous for only having two blocks of public toilets. Contestant: Is it Toulouse?

I didn't get very far in last night's pop quiz. Question 1 was: who invented Tizer…?

Her: 12 across: Iceland's most common bird? Him: Is it frozen chicken?

Him: 10 down: ocean-going, furry creature? Her: Ship's cat, innit?

Her: 16 across: Kentucky derby venue? Him: Try Aintree?

*   *   *

The shout went up, incoming! Next thing, I was hit on the head by a flying pub…

I went on a visit to the Edinburgh Military Tattoo. When I got home, I had C Coy, 13th/18th Royal Hussars, inked across my chest.

Will resigned from the army because the officers kept telling everyone to fire at him…

I was sacked from sniper school when I found I couldn't hit a barn door from six inches. At least no one can say I didn't give it my best shot.

When I joined the army, I was given a yellow uniform with black hoops. Whey hey, I thought: I'm in Bee Company.

This bloke showed me an early morning picture of his granddad in the trenches. I said, shot at dawn? He said, was he heckers like; he won a posthumous VC at the first Battle of Passchendaele!

On the eve of the Battle of Hastings, King Harold was surveying his company of Irish archers, when a misplaced arrow just missed his head. Turning to his corporal, he said, watch him at the battle tomorrow: he'll be taking somebody's eye out with that…

I was offered a job, delivering sausages and meat pies to Catterick Garrison. It wasn't quite what I was looking for; but it was certainly food for fort...

When I was in the army, I ate nothing but ice-cream, lemon meringue and chocolate fudge cake. Yup, I was a desserter...

I had a bad dose of diarrhoea on the morning of my first army parachute jump. Talk about hitting the ground running.

I said to this squaddie, what are you, regular, like? He said, too right I am; you can set your blooming clock by me, that's all...

Field Marshall Rommel went into a greasy spoon. He said, I'll have the full Monty, please.

What did Field Marshall Rommel say to his men just before they got in their tanks? Come on now, lads: get in them tanks!

I heard this noise going: brrr, trickle, left-right, brrr, trickle, left-right. Whey hey, I thought: it's the cold stream guards.

As an ex-Para, I definitely thought my bill for dental treatment was a bridge too far.

*   *   *

All that money and they live like pigs: Pinky and Perky.

I've lost my bank book. If anyone finds it, I strongly recommend the chapter on Barclays.

There's a rumour going round the bank has run out of money. I hope I'm wrong, like, but I think there might be something in it...

I used to be a mean marine. I'm retired nowadays, but I can still peel an orange in my pocket.

I said, doctor, doctor, I come out in an awful rash every time I use the ATM. He said, try not to worry; it's probably just withdrawal symptoms...

I arrived home to discover my mother, crying her eyes out in the middle of a hot flush, while raiding the piggy bank. Oh no, I thought: she's going through the change...

I went cap in hand to the bank manager after the wife spent every penny we had on a job lot of paper, pencils and crayons. He said, overdrawn, eh? I said, what do you think...?

My girlfriend's been made redundant from the bank. Not that she's bothered; she was going to pack it in, anyway. She said there was no money in it.

I walked in this bank, brandishing a Magnum. I couldn't believe how quickly the cashiers dove for cover when confronted with white-chocolate ice-cream on a stick.

I'm not saying the bloke next door is tight; but he's just had double glazing fitted so the kids can't hear the ice-cream van...

It's his fault coins these days are minted with multiple edges. Yup, it's so you can get them out of his hand using a spanner.

When he opens his wallet, the Queen blinks with the light...

*   *   *

I was driving home in my new car when I broke down. I thought, I'll never keep up the repayments...

I went to the shop for a bottle of tomato sauce. Shopkeeper said, HP? I said, no, thanks; I'll be paying cash if it's all the same with you...

I got the kids a BMX each last Christmas and they're still not paid for twelve months later. Honestly, I'm caught up in a right cycle of debt.

So, there I was, walking down the street with my pal, when I spotted this gang of youths, coming up fast from behind. I said, I reckon we're going to get mugged here. He said, I think you might be right…oh, and before I forget, here's that fiver I owe you.

Woman arrives at the council tax office with two £10 notes in her lug 'oles. The shout immediately goes up: Here she comes, look, twenty pound in 'er ears again…

Our kid turned up with this off-colour sea creature; eight arms and a long, thin body, smothered in tentacles. There you go, bro, he said, there's that sick squid I owe you.

Next day, he was in the pub, handing over Spanish opera singer, Placido Domingo. He said, it was a tenor, wasn't it…?

I'm worried the wife might be money laundering. She's just washed my jeans with £20 in the back pocket.

There's this bloke at work called Bob Tanner. Honestly, he hasn't got a Penny to his name.

I'm not saying the missus is a spendthrift; but all she does all day is wander from shop to shop, flashing the plastic, and saying, visa nice, visa'll fit, visa'll do…

I spotted this Great White, counting out tens and twenties on a doorstep. Ooh look, I thought: a loan shark.

* * *

I raced my girlfriend to the camera shop…it was a photo finish.

If someone asked me to list the positives of buying a digital camera, I'd have to say there aren't really any negatives…

News at Ten came on. Newsreader said, and these are tonight's headlines. And the camera zoomed in on his forehead.

I've always been a late developer. I didn't enter adulthood until my late teens. Now bad timekeeping has cost me my job at the photo lab…

Thieves captured on CCTV, stealing 20 tons of wheat from a local farm, as yet remain unidentified. Police have blamed the lack of progress on grainy footage.

In a separate incident, a gang of horned sheep were caught on camera, driving a car through a shop window, before making off with thousands of pound's worth of stock. Police suspect ram raiders are to blame.

Blooming speed cameras are everywhere these days: I've just been flashed twice on my Scalextric.

This motorist waved me down, screaming he'd just run over a pig. I said, what did you do with his speed camera?

I've just seen a snake run over by a motorbike. If you don't believe me, here's a picture: $

A sign outside the hospital said: CCTV in operation. I thought, crikey, let's hope it's not serious…

*   *   *

This bloke told me a joke about a bird. I thought, toucan play at that game…

Owls: they don't give a hoot.

What's the most common owl in Great Britain? A tea towel.

This big, black bird asked me how far it was to the nearest supermarket. I said, about a mile…Asda crow flies.

Someone said there was a decent turn on at the working men's club. When I got there, it was an Arctic sea bird with a big, yellow beak.

I heard this quack-quack, quack-quack noise coming from the bathroom. I think it must have been the toilet duck.

A pal of mine's opened a budgie shop. He says they're going cheep and flying out of the door…

Newsflash: A flock of sick birds has been discovered hiding in the back of a truck on a cross-channel ferry. Customs officers have confirmed they are ill eagle immigrants.

Student: I spent the summer holidays shoving bangers up pigeon's backsides, miss. Teacher: Backsides? Don't you mean rectum? Student: Wrecked 'em? It blew their blooming heads off!

I used to be a parrot, but I'm not now. I used to be a parrot, but I'm not now. I used to be a parrot, but I'm not now. I used to be a parrot, but I'm not now. I used to be a parrot. but I'm not now…

I keep thinking I'm an ostrich. I know I'm going to have to face up to my problem sooner or later. I can't keep burying my head in the sand.

So I said, I'm off on a duck do tonight. He said, what's a duck do, like? I said, quack-quack, quack-quack!

Canary for sale. Going for a song.

* * *

The cat o' nine tails I inherited: I've flogged it.

I wish I'd not bothered now. When I told the wife, there was a right backlash over it.

It all got resolved in the end, though; we bought it back again after organising a bit of a whip round…

Bloke arrives home from the vets with a shovel on a lead. Wife says, what's all this, like? He says, it's the cat: I've had it spade.

What would you get if you crossed a former leader of the Chinese Communist Party with a Persian cat? Chairman Miaow.

The president of the UK Rocky Balboa Appreciation Society was visiting the big cat enclosure at Chester zoo, when part of a sign fell off the wall and knocked him unconscious. Investigations revealed it was the 'I' of the tiger.

I popped to the chemist on Christmas Eve and there was this cat in, waiting for a prescription. Whey hey, I thought: puss in Boots.

So I said, every night, this moggy does its business on my front lawn then digs a hole and buries it. He said, so what? That's what all cats do, isn't it? I said, what, with a shovel…?

I bought a canine plaster-cast modelling kit but must have got the mix wrong, because it finished up looking more like a cat. Yup, it all went purr-shaped.

The wife bought me a new shirt with snarling, Siberian wildcats attached to the bottom of each sleeve. Whey hey, I thought: cuff lynx…

Every night's a night on the tiles for our kid. He's a cat burglar.

Lions that hang around with tigers: haven't they any pride?

*   *   *

Our kid's called his new dog Measles. Bit rash if you ask me.

We lost 1-0 to the dog wardens XI in the 1st round of the cup. Jack Russell got the winner…

I was a bit disappointed with new pop sensations, the Dalmatians: they only did two spots.

I was walking through the park, pondering why I owned the world's most disobedient dog. Then it came to me…

Our kid reckons he threw this stick so far, his dog had to retrieve it from the other side of town. Sounds a bit far-fetched to me.

Bloke goes into the record shop, looking for Prince. Assistant says, do you mean the much lamented, multi-award winning artiste responsible for Purple Rain? He says, no, a flea bitten, black and white mongrel with a brown-studded collar.

Dog fouling is definitely on the increase. I was clean through on goal yesterday, when I was tripped from behind by a rampaging Rottweiler.

I asked this bloke what his American Pit Bull puppies were going for. He said, anything they can get their teeth into...

The dangerous dogs act is a joke. I've just seen a bull terrier, plate spinning, and it broke the blooming lot...

Him: Name a song with a dog in it. Her: Strangers in the Night. Him: Where's the dog in that? Her: Scooby Dooby Doo...

I've called my new dog McCain. I'm having him micro-chipped next week.

*   *   *

Our kid's going out with a limbo dancer. How low can you get?

I'm extremely well-groomed. Yup, I've been married 23 times in 6 years.

A bottle of lemonade proposed to a bottle of dandelion and burdock. It popped the question.

I've been told my ex is back in love again, with a bloke from the dilute orange plant this time. By the sound of things, she's got a right crush on him.

I'm dating a girl from the chewing gum factory. She's not much to look at, like; but I couldn't wish for a more-bubbly personality.

This woman at the bus stop asked what my favourite Elvis record was. I said, are you lonesome tonight? She said, far from it, mister. Now go and work your charm somewhere else!

So I said, I got really drunk at this wedding and knocked the cake over. She said, blimey; how many tiers? I said, how many tears? Blooming bucket loads, that's all.

I popped round to keep big sis company while the builders were in. I said, what are we having for dinner? She said, I've not really thought about it? I said, do you fancy the chippy? She said, not really; but I must confess that sparky is a bit of alright!

Not only is my new girlfriend stunning, she's also a fantastic singer. As if that wasn't enough, she runs her own ceramics business. Her name? Why, it's Bonnie Tiler, of course...

The girl next door's just got engaged to the manager of the back scratcher factory. Well, well, well, I thought: so they're finally getting itched.

I booked us a night in the Ritz for an anniversary surprise. I don't think the wife was too impressed when we finished up spending the night in a box of salted crackers.

My wife-to-be wasn't best pleased when I was late for the wedding rehearsal. She said she didn't know where she stood with me…

After years of being single, I've finally pulled. Yup, I've signed up for the town tug o' war team.

I was going to ask this girl from Moscow to marry me; but I didn't want to Russia.

*   *   *

My cross-eyed girlfriend: I'm sure she's seeing someone else.

I finally confronted the wife over her obsession with Alvin Stardust. She said it was just my jealous mind.

The girlfriend wasn't happy when I called her a Mediterranean. She said, say what you like…but there's no need to use the sea word.

I said to the wife, how do you mean, you swallowed your iPad then mine straight after? She said, blame the doctor: it was him who told me to go home and take a couple of tablets.

After a massive row with the wife, I grabbed my Xbox, IPhone, iPad and iPod, then jumped in the car and didn't stop driving until I reached John O'Groats. When I got back, two days later, she said, you always have to take things too far, don't you?

We were back at it the same afternoon. I said, sticks and stones may break my bones, but words can never hurt me. I wasn't quite so cocky after she'd clobbered me over the head with a hardback version of the Oxford English Dictionary.

I went on the Jeremy Kyle Show when I found out my girlfriend had been cheating. I don't think old Jezza boy was best impressed when I explained it was during a game of Monopoly.

When I came down with a tickly cough, the doctor recommended the wife rub my chest with Vic. It helped the cough, like; but I came out in this awful rash from his stubbly chin.

After another humongous row, the wife sat down on the settee and began sharpening her pencil. I said, there you go again, look; trying to make a point.

I told the wife I'd been diagnosed with insomnia. She said she wouldn't be losing any sleep over it…

*   *   *

The wife and I were really happy for 20 years. Then we met.

When I divorced my wife, she took everything; house; car; money; even the dog. She was the one that got her way…

I was on the roller coaster with the wife. She said, if it turns upside down, do you think we'll fall out? I said, don't be daft: we've been best of friends for thirty years now.

The wife says all I do is lounge around, watching football, and that, if our marriage is to survive the weekend, we need to make time to talk. I thought, yeah, right: like that's going to happen, when I've just settled down to enjoy extended highlights of York City versus Bury in the 2nd round of the Johnstone's Paint Trophy.

When I spotted my ex, speeding towards us in a car full of stolen cash, I grabbed my new girlfriend by the arm and told her not to move. I said, I'll never allow her to drive a wedge between us…

My cousin's marriage to the subsidence engineer is in trouble. Not that I'm surprised. I could see the cracks appearing months ago.

It's not the only marriage that's on the rocks, either. Have you heard about that nice couple that live in the old lighthouse…?

My sister is back single again after calling off her engagement to her candle maker fiancé. She said he didn't half get on her wick.

This just a few months after splitting from her painter and decorator boyfriend. She was sick of him telling her she needed two coats on.

The food hamper I organised for my former wife: I sent it by Fed Ex.

*   *   *

I knocked my brother clean out after hitting him over the head with a chocolate bar. Classic.

I'm setting up a charity for injured chocolate bars: Help for Aeros goes live in the morning.

There's a rumour going round I'm flogging knock-off Mars Bars from Beijing. Don't believe a word: it's all Chinese Wispas.

Did you hear about the fight in the 1970s biscuit tin? A Bandit hit a Penguin over the head with a Club and made a Breakaway in a Taxi.

Driving down this road, I spotted loads of chocolate-coated sweets, waiting for the green man to flash. Whey hey, I thought: a Revel crossing.

I've just seen a coconut-filled chocolate bar on horseback. Dressed like a cowboy, with Stetson, poncho and six-shooters, it was puffing on a cigar and leafing through piles of rolled-up wanted posters. Ooh look, I thought: a Bounty hunter.

I took my chocolate bar back to the shop when it wouldn't stop singing Eminem songs. Apparently it was the rapper.

Police were called to the supermarket to interview a magician's assistant, being held on suspicion of secreting chocolate bars inside his clothing. The manager said he definitely had a few Twix up his sleeve.

Did you see that film last night, the one where earth was invaded by a marauding army of walnut whips? It was called War of the Whirls.

I bought a chocolate teapot but wish I hadn't bothered. It was about as much use as a chocolate teapot.

*   *   *

Everyone thinks I'm playing the part of Santa at the office Christmas party. Little do they know, but I've got the perfect get out Claus…

I told the wife to turn the Christmas lights on. Next thing, she was dressed in her best pink negligée, dancing seductively beside the tree.

Him: I got this brilliant book for Christmas, all about the history of famous Scottish towns. Her: Motherwell? Him: She's bearing up, like; but her lumbago's been giving her a bit of gyp of late.

I hid a stash of dodgy diamonds in my dessert when the law came knocking during Christmas dinner. When the case went to court, I was found guilty as charged. The judge said the proof was in the pudding…

Good King Wenceslas goes into the pizza shop. He says, I'll have a large, stuffed crust Hawaiian, please. Assistant says, deep and crisp, and even, is it...?

I bought the girlfriend a wooden leg for Christmas. It wasn't her main present, like; just a stocking-filler.

Football fans are getting really excited: only three more Leeds United managers till Christmas.

When all I got for Christmas was a bag of boiled sweets, I headed straight for the pub to drown my sorrows. Bar, humbug.

Every Christmas, we get a ghost in the house. I reckon it must be the festive spirit.

He's got the sack. Father Christmas.

*   *   *

Did you hear about the over-zealous referee that went into a hotel and booked all the rooms?

What a brilliant match: it was about an inch and a half long and had a pink, phosphorus head.

Apparently United's new manager has lost the dressing room. Will someone please tell him it's the third door on the left at the bottom of that long corridor?

The Reds haven't looked back since signing a goalkeeper from the launderette football team. They've never kept so many clean sheets...

Caught red-handed, breaking into a Dutch international footballer's car, I was immediately mobbed by hordes of star-struck fans. All I said was: I'm Robbin' Van Persie...

Rumour has it that Rovers are about to unveil a big name signing. Stylianos Stelios Giannakopoulos, of Borussia Mönchengladbach, is expected to put pen to paper soon.

When my rented vehicle broke down outside Old Trafford, I nipped into reception and asked if they could give me Salford Van Hire's telephone number. This woman said, sorry, sir; but contact details for our Dutch international footballers are strictly confidential.

2-0 down, with ten minutes to go, City sent the sub on. The gaffer said, right, let's see how they cope with a nuclear powered hunter-killer…

Animal rights activists are protesting outside Manchester United's training ground after it was revealed Wayne Rooney had injured a calf.

So I said, who's the player with gold stars on each shoulder and a rake of medals pinned to his chest? This bloke said, do you mean the midfield General?

I spotted our kid on telly, causing a rumpus in the away end. I always knew he'd finish up in the wrong crowd...

I fell down this big hole in the penalty area. The referee sent me off for descent.

What's a referee's favourite in-car feature? The trip recorder.

*   *   *

We're having a cricket match on Shrove Tuesday. The toss is at one o'clock.

I booked a trip to Lourdes but got on the wrong bus. England finished the day on 489 for 6.

Pet food giant, Spillers, have pulled out of a deal to sponsor the England cricket team. It was thought they'd look a bit daft with WINALOT on their shirts.

The tax evader's cricket club were 752-2 at close of play. Asked if he was going to declare, the captain said, what do you think…?

What would you get if you crossed a Dutch (impressionist) painter with a fast moving (white) commercial vehicle and a famous (retired) Yorkshire cricketer? Vincent Van Gough.

Two pals at the Test Match. One says, how about we forget this rubbish, book a flight, and drive coast to coast across the States instead? His mate replies, Route 66, like? He says, Root 66? Don't be daft: he was out first ball!

Bloke goes to the doctors with a cricket ball stuck up his backside. Quack says, how's that? He says, don't you start!

I couldn't believe it when I heard our star player had been dropped after falling out with the coach. I thought, how can having an argument with a bus possibly keep him out of the team?

I had a member of the England cricket team round to cut my grass for me. It was Mowin' Ali...

What do you call a world class English cricketer? Retired.

*   *   *

Muhammad Ali figurine for sale. £50 ono. Not boxed.

I've just seen a fight between two vacuum cleaners. Honestly, it was a right old dust up.

My first cage fight didn't go as planned. I was knocked out by a hamster in round one.

That's the last time you'll catch me in the local Spar shop. I went fifteen rounds with some bloke who thought he was Rocky Balboa and returned home with two black eyes and a thick lip.

I bet you didn't know that American hip-hop group, The Black Eyed Peas, used to be known simply as, The Peas. Apparently they had this big argument one day, settled things in the ring, and the rest is history...

Boxer goes to A&E with a broken hand. He said, it's all the bloke next door's fault. He asked me if I'd pop round and help him knock a wall out…

Police were called to the grand opening of Humberside's new Disney Store when a fight broke out over a Jungle Book cuddly toy. Eye witnesses said it was a right Hull-a-Baloo…

The girlfriend dumped me over my obsession with Hollywood boxing films. Not for long, though; we were just going through a Rocky patch.

A fight broke out at the cartoonist and caricature society AGM. A police spokesman confirmed arrests had been made but said details remained sketchy.

So, there I was, having a right old ding-dong with the wife, when a fight broke out between two Germans. She said, do something, then. I said, no way: you'll only accuse me of splitting Herr's…

This sign outside the breaker's yard said: cash paid for scrap. I was back five minutes later with my boxing gloves.

Two nuts walking through the park. One was a salted…

*   *   *

U-bends: I can't get my head round them…

My best friend is Harvey. He adores vodka and orange and makes a living from hanging pictures. Oh, and just in case you wondered, his surname is Wallbanger.

The wife wasn't happy when I told her I was buying a pneumatic drill. New one? she said. And can you please explain what's wrong with the old one?

Mum, dad, grandma, grandad, aunty Pat, uncle Stephen, Paul, Mark, Chris, and fifteen cousins, all joined forces to change a bulb. Many hands make light work.

A builder hit me with a ten grand bill for a new roof. I asked if I could put it on the slate...

There was this brickie in the DIY shop with sticks of dynamite strapped to his backside. Ooh look, I thought: a builder's bomb.

This bloke asked me if there was a B&Q in Wigan. I said, I'm not sure, mate; but there's definitely a W and a G...

Our kid and his girlfriend have moved into a flat above the DIY shop. My dear departed mother would turn in her grave if she knew they were living over the brushes.

I nipped to the shop for a couple of sheets of fine sandpaper, but all they had was multi-packs. Ah well, I thought: sometimes you have to take the rough with the smooth.

A Batman villain with green hair and a painted face turned up to fit my new front door. Whey hey, I thought: a practical Joker.

*   *   *

Humpty Dumpty: he's a right big head.

If you ask me, he's not all he's cracked up to be, either...

Speaking of which, did you hear about the Irish Humpty Dumpty? A wall fell on him.

I've just seen a chicken, splashing around at the sewage works. It was poultry in motion.

Walking past the farm, I heard this rubbish singing coming from the chicken coop. I thought, they'll never make it on the eggs factor.

I answered the phone and this voice went: cluck-cluck, cluck-cluck, cluck-cluck. It was someone calling from Hen Power.

Her: There was this chap at the door earlier, darling, selling chickens and bricklaying equipment. Him: Did you buy anything, dear? Her: Not much, darling: just a few hods and hens.

I wasn't best pleased when I found my hotel room overrun with chickens. Apparently it was hen-suite...

Why did the bubble gum cross the road? Because it was stuck to the chicken's foot.

Why did the film mad chicken cross the road? To see Gregory Peck.

*   *   *

People laugh when I tell them I used to be a farmer. I don't know why: I was outstanding in my field.

I've landed a job, mucking out at the farm. The money's crap, like; but at least it's stable.

The bloke next door reckons he earns £500 per week, hosing down pigs at the farm. If you ask me, it's complete and utter hogwash.

I lost a needle in a haystack. I found it in the end, like; but it was like looking for a needle in a haystack.

I discovered a deep hole, filled with water. Then another. And then another. I thought, well, well, well...

I've just been made redundant from my job at the dairy farm. Yup, I'm off to pastures new.

So I said, freezing cold and I had to work Christmas blooming Day at the farm. It was a good job there was a slap-up dinner with all the trimming to look forward to. He said, pigs in blankets, like? I said, no, but I made sure the sheepdog kept its coat on...

I adore mucking out and my favourite film is Apocalypse Now. I love the smell of the pig farm in the morning...

What does a parrot have in common with a hippopotamus? Neither can drive a tractor.

Come to think of it, I think they'd struggle to milk the cows as well.

*   *   *

Tardis for sale. No time wasters, please.

DIY vasectomy kit for sale. Going for a snip.

For sale: ex-Royal Mail parcel van. Can deliver.

Mo Farah's car for sale. No tax or MOT but good runner…

Parachute for sale. Only used once. Never been opened.

Puppet show free to good home. No strings attached.

Tinchy Stryder figurine for sale. Not rapped.

£5,000 secures autograph by Yoko Lennon. ONO.

For sale: VW Polo. Mint condition.

Sky rocket for sale. Only used once.

*   *   *

A bloke offered me £200 for my pet alligator: it snapped his hand off.

Pushy tape measure salesmen. I can't believe some of the lengths they'll go to.

I used to be the top salesman at the Ford garage. Then I lost my Focus.

A bloke tried to sell me a mountain for £10,000. I told him it was a bit steep.

I went for a Vidiprinter salesman's job but didn't get it. Apparently they were looking for someone results driven…

This insurance salesman called round and immediately demanded we turn our raunchy DVD off. I said, are you from the Prude…?

I said, I got that job at the coal centre. He said, don't you mean call centre? I said, no, coal: all my colleagues are ex-mineworkers.

I went to buy a new car with our kid. This salesman said, gobble-gobble, gobble-gobble. And our kid replied, gobble-gobble, gobble-gobble. I think they were talking turkey.

I resigned from my Veno's salesman's job when my wages weren't paid, two weeks in a row. Apparently there was no money in the coughers.

Boy: Dad, Dad, there's a man at the door with a bald head. Dad: Tell him I've already got one.

I love my new sausage salesman's job, but don't think much to the company car. Honestly, it's a right old banger.

Toilet salesman required: Excellent package and choice of company Carsie…

So I said, that bike you're selling: what's the lowest you'll go on it? He said, two miles per hour. Any slower and you'd fall off.

The North Sea oil salesman next door. Boy, he's slick…

*   *   *

Boy racers: they're the torque of the town.

This bloke tried to sell me a car without an engine. I told him where to shove it.

I gave a lift to this bloke who did nothing but scratch his backside the entire trip. Blooming itch-hiker!

Taxi driver calls base: There's this lorry right up my bumper and it's being driven by a crocodile. Base says: A crocodile? Are you sure? Driver says: Hang on a minute, change that: I think it might be a tail-gator…

I said, I've felt a bit Honda the weather today, darling. She said, don't you mean under, sweetheart? I said, no, Honda; it's been raining Japanese motor cars.

There was this RAC patrolman, crying his eyes out at the wheel. I thought, he's heading for a breakdown…

Our kid called to say his car was stuck in quicksand. I said, I bet you're well cheesed off, aren't you? He said, not really; it's not sunk in yet.

My car broke down, so I rang this emergency number and was informed there was no call out charge. I said, no call out charge? I need someone here in five minutes!

My new 2000cc car swallowed my electric drill, lawnmower, and spanner and screwdriver sets. The wife was right: I should never have bought a tool-eater in the first place.

I was behind this car with the Complete Works of Keats on the rear parcel shelf. It was poetry in motion.

I went to buy some new tyres. Fitter said, Goodyear? I said, not bad, thanks. Now, about these tyres…?

I hate buying new tyres: it's highway rubbery.

*   *   *

I drove past this 24-hour garage. 24-hours later, I drove past again. And, sure enough, it was gone.

This sign on the forecourt said: Max height: 11'9". Blimey, I thought, I bet no one drives off without paying at *Max's* garage.

Back on the road, there was another sign, saying: Max speed: 50. Blooming hummers, I thought: he's fast as well.

So I put the radio on and the DJ was rattling on about Max Bygraves. Crikey, I thought, he's in the cemetery now, paying respect to his victims.

The price of fuel is getting beyond a joke. Two grand it cost today to fill the tank up. Honestly, I rue the day I ever laid eyes on that army surplus, Russian made T-34.

I took the car to the garage. I said, every time it rains, I hear this awful hissing noise. Mechanic said, it sounds like the window vipers to me.

So I said, it's overheating as well. He said, are you sure about that? I said, too right I am. You should have seen it last night: it had fish, chips, mushy peas, three chocolate éclairs and a tub of strawberry ice-cream.

This bloke in the VW garage said, Passat. So I handed him a trilby off the next table. He thanked me kindly and asked if I wanted a Polo.

I stopped at this Jet garage and got stuck in a queue behind two RAF Typhoons and a Singaporean Airlines A380 Airbus.

I was nodding off as I drove home in my new car. It was a VW Borer…

*   *   *

Trainee contortionist required. Must be flexible.

I went home from the fair with the Earl of Cumberland under my arm. I won him on hook a Duke.

I can't stand the ringmaster at the circus where I work. I'm sick of jumping through hoops for him.

Did you hear about the fight at the circus? A clown clobbered the sword swallower then went straight for the juggler…

I've just purchased Alton Towers, Lightwater Valley and Blackpool Pleasure Beach. I got them from the office of fair trading.

More people were flocking to the funeral than attending the village fair. It was obviously a fete worse than death.

I'm not saying I'm unlucky...but I'm the only person I know that's lost his no claims bonus on the Dodgems.

I was at the fair with my mates when the world's tallest man appeared. Gathering us together, he began to recite: one potato, two potato, three potato, four, five potato, six potato, seven potato, more. Whey hey, I thought: it's the big dipper.

Duck goes into the Job Centre. Clerk says, got the perfect job for you, mate: performing duck required at Billy Smart's Circus. Duck says, that's no good for me...I'm a plumber.

I asked this tightrope walker how he survived on minimum wage. He said, I must admit, it's a bit of a balancing act...

I had a right argument with the girlfriend on the big wheel. I said, this is going nowhere. All we're doing is going round in circles.

I got fired yesterday, third night in a row: I'm a human cannonball.

*   *   *

Two fish in a tank. One says, you drive: I'll man the guns.

I didn't get that job at the fishmonger's. I was absolutely gutted.

What did the fishing mad dentist type into his sat nav? Route: canal.

Fishing mad, our kid bought a house on Trent Close as tribute to his favourite venue. Just in case you wondered, I live at 69 Spearmint Rhino Avenue.

I had a brilliant evening at Wigan Casino then finished the night off with a flat fish supper. You can't beat a bit of northern sole...

This label on my new trousers said, 32 leg. I thought, crikey, that would fit four octopuses.

I opened a shelter for abandoned dolphins. All was going great until this jobsworth from the council said it was unfit for porpoise.

I spotted a shoal of yellow dolphins in the supermarket. The poor old dear pushing the next trolley swore blind it was a bunch of bananas!

Speaking of which, what's yellow and invisible? No bananas.

Bloke goes into a tackle shop. He says, can you recommend a good large arbour? Assistant says, I've heard Singapore's well worth a blast.

So I said, I'm thinking of starting a wet fish business. He said, sole trader, like? I said, I was thinking more cod and haddock, actually.

What's yellow and highly dangerous? Shark infested custard.

*   *   *

This bloke asked me how me embroidery classes were going. I said, oh, sew-sew...

I feel like I've known the people at the sky diving club all my life. Down to earth doesn't come into it...

I love a good dust up on a night out round town. Next morning, I'll write a blow by blow account then stick the account in my scrap book...

I enrolled for sleigh-dog-driving classes but couldn't hack it. It was too mush-mush for me.

I went in this craft shop. I said, how much for commercial towing vehicle, Nostromo?

I bought a Star Wars plaster-cast-modelling kit but most have got the mix wrong, because Chewbacca disintegrated as soon as I opened the mould. Not to worry; I suppose it's just the way the Wookie crumbles.

Did you hear about the butcher that took up karate? Every time someone asked for chops, he put them to sleep with a couple of swift blows to the neck...

I had the next door neighbour round, banging my door down at 3 o'clock this morning. Good job I was still up, practising on my bagpipes!

Wife: I need a new hubby. Husband: Don't you mean hobby? Wife: No, I'm divorcing you.

My tap dancing lessons didn't go well. I kept falling in the sink.

*   *   *

I've just booked a holiday to the Far East: Cleethorpes.

I was on holiday in New Orleans when this tram went past, filled with spuds. Ooh look, I thought: a street car named Desiree.

Ok, so I went to Benidorm and forgot to take my sun tan oil. There's no need to rub it in...

The bloke next door arrived home from a trip to Zurich, complaining he couldn't find a pint of John Smith's anywhere and that the view from his hotel room was of the local sewage works. Honestly, I don't think I've ever met anyone so bitter and Swiss-turd...

I went to the travel agents and enquired about holidays to New York. Assistant said, Big Apple? I said, no thanks, I've just had my tea; but I'll take one for later if that's alright...?

So she said, New Jersey's something else. I said, do you really think so? I quite like the colour, but reckon it's a bit long in the sleeves...

After a holiday from hell, I wrote a strongly worded letter to the travel company, then stuck the envelope in a vice and attacked it with a rasp.

When the wife asked what I was doing, I said, what do you think? I'm filing a complaint.

Couple holidaying in the States. He said, fancy a blast down Route 66, dear? Or shall we stay in and listen to my new Frank Sinatra CD instead? She said, it's always what you want to do, isn't it? He said, you've got it: it's My Way or the highway...

After a bout of flu, I headed for the travel agents in search of warmer climes. Assistant said, I'm hearing good reports about Qatar. I said, catarrh? Don't make me laugh: I've got a splitting headache and I'm bunged up like you wouldn't believe!

Two pals, touring Scotland. One says, there's still no sign of the Forth Road Bridge. Mate replies, I'm not surprised. We haven't been over the other three yet.

Fell walking in Cumbria, I bumped into this freezing cold American female pop star. Yup, it was Brrr Linda Carlisle...

I went to the travel agents and asked about cheap flights. They told me to try the darts shop next door.

My lost luggage claim fell on deaf ears. They said I didn't have a case.

*   *   *

I was offered a job in a bubble-gum factory. I told them I'd like to chew it over first...

Five minutes later, I was offered a job in a coal mine. I turned that one down: I thought it was a bit beneath me.

I was offered a job in a teddy bear factory next. I told them to get stuffed.

Then a job on a turkey farm. I told them to get stuffed as well.

Oh, and that idiot doing the hiring at the taxidermy shop...

I went for this chauffeur's job and was told I'd need to be driven. I said, driven? I thought it was me who'd be doing the driving…?

So I said, I got that street cleaner's job, darling. She said, marvellous news, dear. Will you have to go on any training courses? I said, no…the boss says I can just pick it up as I go along.

I received two job offers on the same day, one on a production line and the other in a dismantling yard. I thought, this is it: it's make or break time.

I wrote our kid's personal details on the back of a breeze block for him to take to his job interview; just so he wouldn't forget, like. When the gaffer asked his name, he said, Yorkshire brickworks…

My interview for a job in the auditing department of the men's underwear factory couldn't have gone better. They said I definitely ticked all the boxers.

I applied for an illustrator's job but didn't even get an interview. Ah well, I suppose it's back to the drawing board…

Filling in this application form, I was asked to provide the names of two referees. I plumped for Howard Webb and Pierre Luigi Collina.

I'm not getting my hopes up about my application to the starch factory. Competition is bound to be stiff.

*   *   *

I love for my job at the dilute orange plant. But I can't deny I find it difficult to concentrate.

There's been a right to-do over the leak at the ink factory. Local residents have said it's a right blot on the landscape…

The wife refuses to divulge her duties at the car hooter factory. All I know is this: when she arrives home, she's blooming honking!

I broke into the electric drill factory. Everything was going fine until I heard footsteps behind. Next thing, Bosch...

I've phoned in sick on so many occasions, next time I'm going to have to tell them I've snuffed it.

Gaffer: Let's get this straight: you're seriously trying to tell me you've spent the entire shift in the toilet? Apprentice: Don't blame me, boss: it was you who said I was owed a day in loo...

I applied for a loan to open a jigsaw factory but the bank turned me down. I've been in pieces ever since.

I love my new job at the firework factory. Come to think of it, it's bang on!

Not like the knife factory where I used to work: too many backstabbers.

My first shift at the porridge factory? Gruelling.

*   *   *

I've finally landed a job with no pressure: I repair broken water mains.

It's true: I'm officially a white collar worker. I'm a machine operator at the shirt factory.

Just my luck: first day as a trainee lumberjack and the bus was twenty minutes late. The foreman said, what time do you call this, like? Come on: chop-chop!

I got a job with a Japanese car company, who put me straight out on secondment to the lawnmower factory next door. Talk about Hover worked and Honda paid.

So I said, how's the new architect's job going? He said, not good: the boss ripped up my new skyscraper design and told me to start again. I

said, what, too many flaws, like? He said, not really: it was only twelve storeys high...

Our kid got that job on the supermarket returns desk. Seriously, I take it all back...

I told people for years I worked in a sandpaper factory. Then I found out it wasn't a sandpaper factory, after all. We were making maps of the desert...

I rang the gaffer. I said, I'm just arriving on the south coast now, boss. He said, do you realise it's five in the morning? And what are you doing on the south coast? I said, just what you said, boss: making sure I was in Brighton early.

The girlfriend was cock-a-hoop after landing a job as a magician's assistant. I just hope she's not under any illusions, that's all...

I was offered a job as a target erector at the local archery club. I said, I think I'll give that one a miss.

My new lift operator's job: I've promised the gaffer I'll take it to the next level...

I said, why the vacant look? He said, it's my new job: I'm a toilet attendant.

I've landed a job with 50,000 people under me: I cut the grass in the cemetery.

* * *

I've just packed in my window cleaning round. I was forever losing my rag.

My job at the glue factory: I've told them where to stick it.

This after I lost my job at the snuff factory: I was sacked for pinching.

I've just resigned my position as a lift engineer. It wasn't the worst job in the world, like; but it certainly came with its fair share of ups and downs…

I've just been sacked from my job in the R&D department at the crisp factory. Not that I'm surprised. I've never exactly been flavour of the month.

As for our kid, well…he's only been suspended from his job at the lawn mower factory, hasn't he? They've gone and stuck him on blooming gardening leave!

I got a job as a trainee hangman but walked out after an hour. There was no one around to show me the ropes…

I was so sick of life at the call centre that I chopped the equipment to pieces with a machete. I've since been charged with phone hacking.

When I resigned, the boss offered me the earth to stay. He wasn't kidding, either. I got home and there was a ton of top soil on the drive.

I've just resigned from the colander factory. I couldn't take the strain anymore.

My acupuncturist job: I'd pack it all in for two pins.

*   *   *

Horses: they live for donkey's years!

Hot tip for the 3.35 at Aintree: Dusty carpet: never been beaten.

I've just bought a racehorse, 25-hands high. I'll let you know how I get on.

At the reading of the will, I was bequeathed a redundant pit shaft, while the lady opposite finished up with two donkeys. I said, I'll show you mine, if you show me Eeyore's…

I went to bed with a tickly cough and woke next morning with four legs, a swishy tail, pointed ears and a thick mane of hair down the back of my neck. When the wife asked if I was any better, I said, not bad...I'm just feeling a bit horse, that's all.

This clerk at the Job Centre said I'd lose my dole money if I didn't go on a few courses. So I spent a full week at Ascot, Epsom and Haydock Park...

This lettuce recommended I back this horse and the little beauty came in at 100/1. Talk about tip of the Iceberg...

Our kid was arrested after formulating a cure for acne then quadrupling the proceeds at the bookies. He's since been charged with spot fixing.

I bet this bloke a tenner he couldn't go to sleep on a window-sill and he only went and did it! What a ledge!

There was this I know bloke at the bookies, laughing his head off in the middle of a severe bout of palpitations. Bless him; he always did enjoy a bit of a flutter...

I used to be in an elite cavalry unit. Special horses, actually.

What's black and white and eats like a horse? A zebra.

*　　*　　*

This cowboy asked if he could borrow $20. Whey hey, I thought: Skint Eastwood!

I bumped into Billy the Kid on his way into the bank. I said, fancy a chat, Billy? He said, I'd love to; but unfortunately I've got to shoot...

I went to this wedding and was immediately introduced to a whooping woman in buckskins with feathers in her hair. Apparently it was the chief bridesmaid.

Geronimo goes into this restaurant. Waiter says, do you have a reservation, sir? Geronimo says, no, I live in a council flat on Kings Road.

Rumour has it Richard Branson is bidding to take over the running of UK-wide council bin collections after his son said he wanted a cowboy outfit for his birthday.

Did you hear about the paper cowboy? He had a paper hat; paper waistcoat; paper shirt; paper trousers and paper boots. He even had a paper gun and holster. They hung him for rustling.

I'm moving to the Wild West to start a new life as a Cheyenne Indian dog soldier. My parents aren't happy, like; but at least they're putting a Brave face on it.

I wasn't impressed when Butch Cassidy and the Sundance Kid turned up to start work on my new extension. I thought, that's all I need: cowboy blooming builders!

Cowboy walks into a German car showroom and shouts: Howdy! Salesman replies: No Audis here, mate; but I can do you a cracking deal on a BMW.

I've just received a letter from Sitting Bull's solicitor. I thought, I can't believe it: I'm being Siouxed!

*   *   *

I went out dressed as Sir Lancelot and didn't get home till six in the morning. Talk about night in shining armour...

I resigned my reporter's job then bought a battle horse and a suit of armour and went on tour, performing complimentary jousting exhibitions. I always promised myself a bash at free-lancing.

Sir William Wallace and clan must have had terrible skin in the film, Braveheart. Who can forget the bit when he raises his sword and says, they make take our lives; but they'll never take our...Freederm!

Mobile phones have been around longer than people think. I was watching this film the other night and distinctly heard Sir Lancelot tell someone to fetch his charger.

I went for a bite to eat at two in the morning and discovered this café, filled with blokes in suits of armour. Whey hey, I thought: an all-knight diner.

I was chased from the waxworks by a woman with a rapier in one hand and a claymore in the other. Apparently it was Madame Two Swords.

I arrived at the sports centre with a roll of wire, a box of nails and two dozen wooden posts. I said, right, which way to the Olympic fencing trials…?

We invited a bloke in a suit of armour round for supper and he didn't utter a word all evening. It was a good job we fancied a quiet knight in…

Outside the castle, the peasants were revolting. And those inside weren't too pretty, either!

I saw a swordfight on the way into work. It was on a duel carriageway.

*   *   *

Last night's documentary about sentry duty at Buckingham Palace. Out-standing.

On a visit to Buckingham Palace, I noticed loads of activity in the kitchen area. Ooh look, I thought: they're changing the lard.

This bloke said, I'm going to offer Prince William's brother a tenner to put me a good word in with Kate Middleton's sister. I said, but that would be bribe Harry!

I went to the Tower of London and sat, bemused, watching half a dozen Beefeaters, eating salad sandwiches.

When everyone complaining of a sore throat, commentators and bookmakers alike were forced to agree this year's London Marathon would be a too-hoarse race.

There was one runner dressed as a chicken and another dressed as an egg, neck and neck at the finish of the London Marathon. I thought, hmmm, now this *is* going to be interesting…

I've heard there are loads of jobs going begging in London. Trouble is, who'd want to be a beggar? And, more to the point, who'd want to live in blooming London!

Historians have discovered the headstone of the world's oldest man on the M1 near Sheffield. Apparently was 162 and his name was Miles from London.

When I was in the army, I got lost in London. I was missing in Acton.

Big Ben: you wouldn't want to mess with him.

*   *   *

My pet mouse, Elvis…he's been caught in a trap.

Our kid bought a pile of old vinyl off eBay. I said, let's have a Decca...

Went to watch a band called Prevention. Have to say they were better than The Cure.

This bloke was boasting how he saved an ageing rock star's life, dragging him to safety after finding him dangling over the edge of a cliff. I said, was he in dire straits, like? He said, Rolling Stones, actually; but that's another story...

Bloke goes to the quacks. He says, doctor, doctor, I can't stop singing Johnny Cash songs. Doctor says, Ring of Fire? He says, not really; not since that dodgy curry last week, anyway…

Peter Andre's UK fan club are said to be devastated by reports the Australian heart-throb has a new love interest: a woman who's always crying and looks like Red Rum. Equally upsetting is news he's written a song about her: Miss Teary Horse Girl is due for release next week.

Whenever it's nice out, there's this American pop duo that hang around on street corners, giving money away. Yup, it's Sunny and Share.

Him: What's your favourite Lulu song? Her: Shout. Him: I said what's your favourite Lulu song! Her: Shout! Him: What's your favourite Lulu song!!! Her: Shout, ******* Shout!!! Him (mumbling): Deaf *******! Her (muttering): Stupid ****!

What do you call a bloke with Roger Daltrey stuffed up one nostril and Pete Townshend up the other? Who nose...?

I've got tickets to see a group called Sumo Wrestlers. Apparently they're really big in Japan.

This copper asked if I had a police record. I said, ar, Walking On the Moon...

* * *

I'm not saying our kid's obsessed with the army, but he's only gone and christened his new born twins, Milly and Terry.

This a few weeks after he changed his name to Col, so that people would think he was a high-ranking army officer.

The chap next door called his boys Eton and Harrow. Then again, he always was old school.

There was this woman, showing off her new baby boy. And the poor little mite only had a hand! I said, what's his name, like? Danny...?

I rang the surgery after my kid brother, Darren, woke up thinking he was a box of washing powder. I said, can I make an appointment, please...it's for our Daz.

I couldn't afford a private number plate, so I did the next best thing and changed my name by deed poll. From now on, I'd appreciate it if you'd refer to me as: P136 CTH.

I was only a day old when this kid in the next cot tried to sell me a dodgy rattle. I said, do you think I was born yesterday...?

The mother-in-law was adamant our new born baby had my eyes. I said, if that's the case, can you please explain how they're still in my head?

I was shocked to discover my new born baby only had an ear. I said, will it lead a normal life, doctor? He said, I'm afraid not: it's deaf.

Our second child was born nine months later and only had a head. Poor kid, he hated Christmas and birthdays: all he ever got was hats.

He was in a terrible mood the day he had his teeth out; but it wasn't all bad news. When he started school, he was immediately named head boy.

This bloke offered me a tenner to change my name to Eisenhower. I told him to take an Ike.

I said, it's not fair. He said, what's not? I said, my new ginger-haired baby.

*   *   *

The girlfriend wasn't impressed when I gave her a camel for her birthday. She didn't half get the hump on.

I got a wok for my birthday but absolutely despise Chinese food. No worries, though; I've put that much weight on of late, I can always use it to iron my shirts in.

This delivery driver turned up with the wife's birthday present gripped between his thighs. It's the last time I'll be ordering anything on loin, I can tell you.

The wife wasn't kidding when she promised to take me on a hot air balloon ride for my birthday; a fortnight later, we were still up there. She said, see, I told you I wouldn't let you down, didn't I...?

Bloke takes his watch to the jewellers. He says, I've got a problem with one of the fingers. Assistant says, second hand, I take it? He says, it is heckers like: I got it brand new last birthday!

It was so nice of everyone to sing happy birthday to me as I was escorted from the factory. Special mention goes to the gaffer for giving me my cards...

I gave the girlfriend a tablet for her birthday. She took it next morning after one glass too many down the Dog & Duck.

I bought the wife Andy Capp's autobiography for her birthday; but she wasn't impressed. She said there was no Flo to it...

I'm not saying I'm getting old, like; but when they lit the candles on my cake, I was beaten back by the flames.

It's getting so bad, in fact, I've started giving my age in dog years...

*   *   *

I was caned so many times at school, I started to think my name was Ben Dover.

Teacher: If you had $32,000 in one hand and $32,000 in the other, how much would you have? Pupil: That's the $64,000 question.

This kid on the bus asked if I could help with his biology homework. I said, what's it about, like? He said, the dietary requirements of common house spiders. I said, have you tried looking on the web?

Woman gets on the phone to the education authority. She says, can you recommend a decent public school? Receptionist says, Eton? She says, I've just had my cornflakes, thanks. Now, can you recommend a decent public school...?

Teacher: Can anyone spell the word, farm? Pupil: Is it E-I-E-I-O, sir? Teacher: E-I-E-I-O? How do you make that out? Pupil: Old MacDonald had a farm, E-I-E-I-O.

First night at a public school and I couldn't get to sleep because of a small, wire-haired pooch, yapping away in the next dormitory. I thought, that's all I need: a boarder blooming terrier...

I went to enrol my kid at school. I said, you don't throw pupils in the river, do you? Because I'm not sending a child of mine anywhere that still practises streaming.

There was this park bench, sitting behind a desk at parents evening, marking exercise books. Ooh look, I thought: it's the new form teacher.

How did Father Christmas do at school? Not bad, actually; he passed all his ho-ho-ho levels.

Dentist: So, how did you chip the tooth? Boy: I did it eating my dinner money, mister.

*   *   *

This surgeon stitched me up. Then he sold me a duff car.

It was red hot the day the plastic surgeon moved in next door. Fifteen minutes later, he'd melted...

I went to casualty after being shot up the Khyber with a pellet rifle. Nurse said, smart arse, like? I said, what do you think...?

The bad news is the wife's been rushed to hospital after eating a motorised road sweeper. The good news is she's picking up nicely.

I adore my new stretcher-bearers job. I'm just trying not to get carried away, that's all.

When I received a text, saying the girlfriend was in Casualty, I rushed straight home, stuck the telly on and didn't move for half an hour. There were plenty of pretty nurses, like; but no sign of the missus. So I got my coat back on and went to the pub instead.

I made a beeline for A&E after hearing rumours they were giving iPads away. I felt such a plonker on the bus home with a plastic patch over each eye.

This bloke asked how much I'd paid for a job lot of NHS bed linen. I said, five hundred sheets...

I went for an X-ray and was informed I'd got a Shadow on my stomach. I said, how the *heck* did Hank Marvin get in there...?

Our kid is such a pessimist. He went for a medical and guess what? His blood test came back B negative.

I spotted this silver birch in green-scrubs, heading for theatre. Ooh look, I thought: a tree surgeon.

A youth near us has overdosed on curry powder. Last I heard, he'd slipped into a korma.

I used to be an ambulance, but I'm not now, wow, wow, wow, wow, wow...

*   *   *

I said, doctor, doctor, I can't stop sighing with relief. He said, you're obviously a man of phew words.

I put cough mixture in my doctor's coffee when he wasn't looking. I thought it was time he had a taste of his own medicine.

I forgot to put the lid on the cough mixture and next morning it was swimming with bluebottles. Whey hey, I thought: a Veno's fly trap.

Bloke arrives at the quacks with rock n roll classic, Milk and Alcohol, blasting from his iPod. Receptionist says, Dr Feelgood? He says, how should I know? Anyway, it's me I'm here about, not him!

Quack: So, you no longer think you're this big Egyptian river? Patient: Well, maybe just a bit. Quack: Try not to worry: it sounds to me like you're in de-Nile.

So I said to the quack, you know how I thought I was a caravan? Well, I still think I'm a caravan; but this one's got wheels on it. He said, and how do you feel about that? I said, blooming ex-static!

I said, doctor, doctor, I can't stop thinking I'm the Boston Strangler. He said, get a grip, man!

I went to the surgery, complaining of double vision. Doctor Hourihane and Doctor Hourihane couldn't have been more understanding.

I said, doctor, doctor, I keep thinking I'm a werewolf. He said, how long's this been going on? I said, quite a while noooooooooow!

Speaking of which, I went to a Halloween party in normal clothes and told everyone I'd come as a werewolf. This bloke said, you don't look much like a werewolf to me. I said, it's not my fault there's not a full moon, is it...?

I've developed suicidal tendencies since coming out all over in horrible, itchy red spots. No cause for concern, though; I'm not about to do anything rash...

I went to the surgery, complaining of recurrent squelching noises and the sound of towels being squeezed out. The doctor said it was probably just a bit of wringing in the ear.

The quack couldn't stop laughing when I told him I was feeling distinctly off it after coming out in short and curlies all over my backside. He said, this is ill-hairy-arse...

I said, doctor, doctor, my social life has been non-existent since I started thinking I was a snail. He said, try coming out of your shell a bit more.

Alright, so my OCD's getting worse. At least I'm still ticking...

*   *   *

Writing a novel without punctuation wasn't easy. I had to pull out all the stops.

I'm writing a follow up to War and Peace but wish I'd never started. Honestly, it's like writing War and Peace…

They say everyone's got a book in them. I know I have: I've just scoffed post-apocalyptic science fiction adventure *Global Kingdom* by *Gary Rowley*.

So I said to this literary agent, I've got a fantastic idea for a book. He said, can you put it in writing?

Author: I'm writing this sweeping epic about a battalion of British soldiers, charging across no-man's-land with fixed bayonets. Agent: Sounds a bit over the top to me.

Set in the golden days of slapstick comedy, my debut novel has become an international bestseller. Things are going great; I just need to make sure I don't rest on my Laurels…

Our kid's written a horror story about a psychopathic wind turbine. Granted, it sounds a bit far-fetched; but the first draught sent shivers down my spine.

I'm writing a book about American motorcycle gangs. I'm currently on the 98th chapter.

Speaking of which, I bought this imitation American motorcycle. It was a Hardly Davidson.

Oh, and I've finally finished my book on English herb gardens. I know, I know, I know: not before thyme…

*   *   *

I took my pet frog to the library. Every time I showed it a book, it went, reddit, reddit, reddit…

My workmates were green with envy when I told them the wife spent the best part of a decade on page 3. I don't know why: she says it's the worst book she's ever read.

I went to the doctors after reading Beau Geste 106 times. He said it sounded like a chronic case of Legionnaire's disease.

I went to the quacks. I said, doctor, doctor, I'm obsessed with glossy magazines. My garage, spare bedroom, wardrobe and the cupboard under the stairs are crammed with thousands of the infernal things. He said, no doubt about it: you've definitely got a few issues…

The M1 is closed after a lorry load of Cinderella DVDs collided with a lorry load of books by Hans Christian Anderson. Police have described the situation as Grimm.

I bought a book called Greenwich Mean Time but wish I hadn't bothered. Talk about daylight robbery.

A headline in the local rag said: 300 Jobs in Jeopardy. So I got on my bike and went to put my name down. That was three weeks ago and I still haven't found the flipping place…

A pal of mine gave me 600 back issues of Smash Hits. With friends like that, who needs NME's?

I watched this brilliant film last night called Lord of the Rings. It was so good, in fact, I might nip down to WH Smith's later and see if the book is out yet.

I'm proud to say I'm in the Guinness Book of Records. Yup, I've drunk more of the black stuff than anyone else in our village.

I said, doctor, doctor, every time I buy a book, I'm only interested in the last few pages. He said, I can't say for sure, but I'm not ruling out appendixitis…

The bloke next door hasn't said much about his new job, flogging advertising space for the local paper. All I can get out of him is that it's classified.

I'm due in court later after being caught breaking into the library. You watch: they'll throw the blooming book at me.

My new girlfriend is called Paige and she reads a new book every day of the week. Just in case you wondered, her surname is Turner.

Our kid reckons he's opening a second-hand bookshop. But I wouldn't take it as read…

*   *   *

I took my PC back to the shop when it wouldn't stop swearing. I said, I think it might be the curser…

I've just put my laptop in hibernation mode. It's currently in a cardboard box under the stairs, covered in straw and scrunched up newspapers.

I got on the phone to my internet provider, complaining my keyboard was covered in chopped pork and jelly again. This bloke said, I think there might be a problem with your Spam filter, sir…

Travelling at the speed of light, I smashed through this PC monitor and went skidding across Mr & Mrs Mitchard's living room floor in Midsomer Norton. It's the last time you'll catch me on the information super highway, I can tell you.

I got the shock of my life when the girlfriend rang to say the computer had crashed. I said, crashed? I didn't even know it had sent off for its licence!

The boss called pest control after someone said they'd seen a mouse in the office. Next morning, we'd caught 22 of the infernal things…all on desks beside computers.

I arrived home to find my PC immersed in a sink full of soapy water. I don't think 'er indoors quite got it when I asked her to wash the windows.

I sold my laptop and bought a Mac instead. Granted, I can't get on the internet anymore; but it doesn't half keep me dry in the rain.

Quack: Antibiotics? What? There's nothing wrong with you, man! Patient: They're not for me, Doc, they're for my computer: it's got a virus.

I entrede a spede tipyng centost adn wno wtih sxi hendrud wrods purr munite.

*   *   *

I bought a hand grenade online. It cost me a bomb.

I ordered this book off the web, all about recent advances in prosthetic limb production. It wasn't cheap, mind; arm and a leg didn't come into it.

Our kid went online and ordered sixteen blue films and twenty travel guides. When they all arrived at once, he said he didn't know if he was coming or going.

I was asked to submit an article for an online discussion. Unfortunately, I'd nothing forum…

I've been trying to sell a stuffed Arabian stallion online for two years now. It's like flogging a dead horse.

I ordered a train set online. Free carriage, it said in the advert. When it came, though, it wasn't with free carriage; but they were good enough to let me off with the postage!

My next door neighbour was pegged out with the washing, while on the phone to the bookies again. Honestly, him and his on-line gambling...

I bought a job lot of hangman's nooses, then quadrupled my investment by selling them one at a time on EBay. Talk about money for old rope.

I ordered a cross trainer online. Big mistake. All it does is shout and lose its temper with me.

This book arrived from Amazon. It was delivered by an illegal logger in a canoe.

*   *   *

I accidentally set fire to my anorak...now it's a blazer.

I set fire to my trousers next. I always did fancy a pair of flares.

I'm thinking of becoming a fireman. I've heard it's a right Bobby's job.

Did you hear about the fireman that moved in next door to a pyromaniac? Things were a bit frosty to start; but now they're getting on like a house on fire.

Speaking of which, I once went to a Scottish pyromaniac's housewarming party. Never again, I can tell you: the theme was Burns Night...

I was lucky to keep my job after setting fire to the trouser factory. I seriously thought I'd burned my britches...

United's decision to sign a former Hollywood stuntman paid off when he scored a hat-trick on his debut. Apparently he was on fire...

I couldn't believe it when my sleeve went up in flames while making dinner. As if things weren't bad enough, the police turned up and charged me with possession of a fire arm.

Her: There's a funny smell coming from the gas fire, darling. Him: Flue trouble, like? Her: Hardly; I had the sniffles the day before yesterday, but that's about it...

Driving instructor: What gear are you in? Pupil: The same as I had on last night. What did you expect, anyway? Helmet, gloves and fire-resistant overalls?

This driving instructor told me to ease off the accelerator and depress the clutch. So I said, accelerator, you're not a bad old stick. Clutch, you make for lousy gear changes. Oh, and in case you're wondering, that smelly brown stuff on my shoe: it's dog pooh!

He told me to let the clutch out next. So I did: I opened the door.

* * *

The drug trafficker whose bike got nicked: he's back pedalling...

Apparently there's an armed siege taking place at the ice-cream parlour. Police have coned off the area.

Did you hear about the bloke who was arrested for squirting Domestos all over the fresh fruit display at the supermarket? He was charged with bleach of the peach.

The pet shop was broken into last night. Police have found a metal chain, tied around a lamppost: they think it might be a lead.

My first day driving the hearse didn't exactly go as planned. I was stopped for undertaking.

Police are on high alert after a masked intruder burst into the supermarket and blasted boxes of Shreddies, Weetabix and Cornflakes with a shotgun. It's feared a cereal killer may be on the loose...

Our kid was arrested after a pallet of washing up liquid went missing from the distribution centre where he works. He reckons he can account for his whereabouts; but the police have said his claims are nothing but a Fairy story.

I bumped into this rough-looking copper, complaining he'd lost his car, contact lenses and handcuffs. I thought, I'll bet he doesn't take any prisoners...

Curators of the National Railway Museum are said to be devastated after the Flying Scotsman went missing overnight. Police are investigating multiple lines of enquiry.

I was arrested after clobbering a bloke over the head with a paving slab. I know, I know, I know: I should learn to kerb my temper.

*   *   *

East End mob rule: it was all the Krays.

I used to be a burglar in Seoul. I was a Korea criminal.

The theft at the badge factory: don't try and pin it on me.

It said on the back of this van: Mob: 07971491017. So I rang it for a laugh. Ten minutes later, I had the Sicilian Mafia, banging the back door down.

Suffice to say, I was more than a bit concerned when I answered the door to this Mafia hit man, asking if he could take my daughter out…

I've become mixed up with a gang of ladder thieves. My mother always said I'd end up in the rung crowd.

I've just had plod round, asking questions about a lorry load of missing breeze blocks. I was absolutely bricking myself…

Apparently police have unearthed a huge stash of cocaine, heroin and ecstasy behind the Job Centre. What a shocker: I didn't even know we had a Job Centre!

Noticing the pub landlord was a bit down in the dumps, I decided to lift his spirits. I nipped down the cellar and made off with a crate of vodka and six bottles of Jack Daniels.

Youth goes on the Antiques Roadshow, showing off a rare Ming Dynasty vase. Presenter says: This is worth twenty thousand pounds. Can I ask where you got it from? Youth says: It was passed down to me, mate. Presenter says: Passed down to you from where? Youth says: From this bedroom window…

Burglars ran riot in a litter bin factory overnight. Apparently they absolutely trashed the place.

I got a phone call from my neighbour, saying there was a burglar in my house, making off with my Walt Disney collection. I said, I hope you're taking the Mickey? He said, I'm not, mate...but I think you'll find *he* is!

My life of crime is finally over. There was only so much I could take...

Someone stole a wheel off my car. I went blooming spare.

*　　*　　*

The Birdman of Alcatraz: I bet they watched him like a hawk.

First night in the nick, I reported a fault with my cell door: there was no handle on the inside.

I shared a cell with a couple of geezers in Parkas, singing Who songs, while talking Vespa's all night. Talk about all the Mod-cons.

This hotel porter screamed: Run, quick! There's an escaped prisoner coming down in the lift! I said: Stop being so con-descending!

I kicked off my singing career with a Johnny Cash style gig at the local prison. It wasn't my best performance, like; but nobody can deny I had a captive audience.

I went to court, charged with possession of a lorry load of stolen hay. I was released on bale…

Paddy, the electrician, refused to touch the malfunctioning electric chair at the prison where he worked. He said that, in his professional opinion, it was a flipping death trap.

I went to court, accused of marrying two women at the same time. Don't ask me why I did it: I suppose I thought it would be really bigamy.

I broke into this Saudi Arabian cosmetics shop, specialising in stick-on eyelid hair. I got a hundred lashes…

Fresh out of prison, I was caught red-handed, secreting a vacuum cleaner up my nostril. I said, blame my parole officer: it was him who told me to keep my nose clean…

I'm up in court tomorrow, charged with spraying graffiti all across town. I think it's fair to say the writing is on the wall…

Did you hear about the bloke who got life for strangling a Smurf, then was released on a technicality? Papa Smurf was furious when he heard: he said he'd get away with blue murder…

I was asked if I'd learned anything from my time behind bars. I said, ar, don't get caught!

I stole a calendar. I got 12 months.

*   *   *

I've set up a plant hire company. If anyone's interested, Yuccas are only a fiver a week.

My itching powder company continues to go from strength to strength. And just to think, I started it all from scratch.

Our kid's gone into business, reading Tarot cards. I wish him well, like; but I can't see him making much of a prophet…

When he's not playing practical jokes on people, the bloke next door makes his living buying and selling hand-operated cuckoo clocks. Wind-up merchant doesn't come into it.

Opening a pork scratchings factory wasn't the best move I've ever made. In actual fact, I made a right pig's ear of it.

I invested every penny I had in a job lot of exercise books, but went bust in a fortnight. There was no margin in them…

It's been officially announced that, with regret, the Blackpool Deckchair Company has now folded.

I understand how the owners must be feeling. I once ran an origami correspondence courses. That folded as well.

I once owned a company called Discount Firing Squad Services. It went to the wall.

I started up a trap door company next. All was going great; but then the bottom fell out of it.

*　　*　　*

I was going to invest in a Chinese distillery but decided against it. Whisky business.

I bought shares in an underwear company instead. Yup, I've got a vested interest.

That said, I wish I'd thought twice before investing my life savings in a job lot of dodgy toilet seats. Talk about a bum deal…

A pal of mine invested in a water wings company. It's up to him, I suppose: he'll either sink or swim.

I've pulled my investment in the crystal ball company. I couldn't see any future in it…

Our kid's only gone and sunk a fortune into a disused mineshaft. Don't ask me why; I don't think I'll ever get to the bottom of it.

The local water treatment company is in financial trouble…according to a leaked memo.

I've just blown ten grand on a job lot of Velcro, sellotape and superglue. I haven't told the wife yet: I just hope she sticks by me.

I'm making loads of lolly. I'm a production manager at the ice-cream factory.

Not nearly as much as my brother at the crisp factory, mind: he's on a right blooming packet.

*   *   *

What did former PM's Harold Wilson and Ted Heath have in common? They both smoked a pipe except for Ted Heath.

I've formed a political splinter group: we're all ex-MP's with little pieces of wood wedged down the back of our finger nails.

It's been on the news that sales of houmous and taramasalata have fallen dramatically. Experts are blaming a double dip recession.

I bought this book about political misinformation during the cold war. Don't ask me what it's like, like: I haven't had a proper gander yet.

As a result of the worsening economic climate, I've finally fulfilled my lifetime's ambition and become an artist. Yup, I'm drawing the dole...

It's been announced that the PM's scalp is infested with mites' courtesy of the Downing Street parrot. That's Polly-ticks for you.

I put the news on and there were loads of snakes, slithering in and out of 10 Downing Street. Whey hey, I thought: a Cobra meeting.

The politicians' Christmas Eve nativity play had to be cancelled when organisers couldn't find anyone to play the parts of the three wise men.

Strolling on the pier, I spotted a long line of politically correct activists, taking a leak in the surf. It must have been the pee-sea brigade.

I booked this free demo: ten minutes later, 2000 people with placards and loud hailers were protesting outside the Town Hall.

This bloke asked who I thought should be centre forward of the parliamentary football team. I said, it would have to be Ed Balls...

Is Brexit what happens when a fat bloke sits on a rickety chair...?

I don't get these calls for an EU benefits cap. Nobody offered me any free hats when I was on the dole...

Teacher: Can anyone define the word, geriatric? Boy: Is it three goals by a German footballer, Miss?

I was staggered when I heard the UK's population was predicted to rise to 80 million by 2030. I thought, what, by half past eight tonight!

My name is Jerzy. I come from Warsaw. I enrolled at the local Polish club. But my first visit was definitely my last. It was filled with weird English people, drooling over tins of Mr Sheen and Kiwi cherry blossom.

So I said, I've just been offered a French rugby union contract. He said, Toulouse? I said, is it heck to lose. This time next year, we'll be lifting the Heineken Cup!

Three blokes in a row asked me if I knew the way to the nearest mental hospital. Blooming asylum seekers...

That German barber near me is a real dab hand. You'll find him in the directory under: Herr Cut.

Did you hear about the Dutchman who fell into a vat of dandelion and burdock? He popped his clogs.

Him: The situation in Greece is a bit worrying, isn't it? Her: Tell me about it. Whatever Sandy saw in Danny blooming Zuko is beyond me!

Teacher: What do you get from ancient Greece? Pupil: Is it ancient chips, Miss?

I went to Paris to see the Mona Lisa. Trust me, she's no oil painting...

I went on the German version of the Apprentice: I got feuered.

*   *   *

I saw this bloke on his way out of the church, covered in spaghetti and tomato sauce. I think it must have been the local pasta.

There was this priest, chasing a trio of blokes in devil costumes round the athletics field. He was obviously exercising a few demons.

I went to this christening and the church roof went up in flames. Talk about a baptism of fire.

Did you hear about the agnostic, dyslexic, insomniac that lay awake every night, wondering if there was a Dog…?

The vicar arrived for Sunday morning service in his best Scooby Doo outfit. Whey hey, I thought: a blessing in disguise.

The Atheist's XI have drawn Manchester United in the 3rd round of the cup. If you ask me, they haven't a prayer…

I had my pea shooter confiscated on the way into church. The vicar said it was a weapon of mass disruption.

So I said, doctor, doctor, I keep thinking I'm Moses, climbing Mount Sinai. He said, go straight home and take these tablets…

I've just seen an eagle, reading a bible. Ooh look, I thought: a bird of pray.

This vicar sold me a mobile phone. It was a pray as you go.

*   *   *

Bloke doing the crossword: Sixteen across: overworked postman? Wife says: How many letters? He says: Two great big sacks full…

I received this letter through the post, offering me a free trial. I turned it down, of course; knowing my luck, they'd only find me guilty.

The missus jumped a mile when a world war one fighter ace suddenly popped through the letterbox. I said, calm down, darling: it's only a flyer…

I went to the post office and mailed myself home in a padded envelope. Bouncing around in the back of a van, I got this call from the wife, asking how long I'd be. I said, trust me; I'll be back in a jiffy…

After scooping a cool £10 million on the Lotto, I was asked what I was going to do with all the begging letters. I said, keep sending 'em!

The letterbox rattled and this eight-foot length of six-by-four landed with a resounding thump on the carpet. I shouted, the post has arrived, darling…

I used to be a postman in China, but got fed up of rowing out to sea to deliver all the junk mail.

On a related topic, what do you think to the news coming out of China: 朣楷琴执窒执璗泂牡橾擝匼峇执窒执猥泂牡橾敬瑪瀰絸朣杢傻执猥扛捡杔淵湀潤渾攆眕咚咚胧慢正牧晙犎梋愗攽敷止憪榢湶楬皵牡氫晥牦浯幨幨幨潴捥捥捥戻捡杔淵湀浩条…

Pat was short-cutting across the football field when a misplaced shot clipped his mail sack before bobbling agonisingly over the goal line. It went in…off the post.

What will they call Postman Pat when he retires? Pat.

*   *   *

I turned down that job at the chippy. I had other fish to fry.

McDonalds drive through: it's like talking to a brick wall.

I've just seen a cheeseburger, driving a Lamborghini. Ooh look, I thought: fast food.

Delivery driver walks into the medical centre and slams a dozen pizzas on the counter. He says, and before anyone asks, it's just what the doctor ordered…

Breaking news: Pizza shop owner discovered dead, covered in pepperoni, cheese, ham and pineapple. Police think he may have topped himself.

So I said, bang a pizza in the oven, darling, then we'll put that gangster film on. She said, Goodfellas, you mean? I said, I was thinking more Chicago Town, like; but if that's all you've got…

Honestly, the looks I got when I crashed my car into McDonalds, demolishing half the restaurant, before skidding to halt at the counter. I said, don't blame me: it's you that's got the sign outside saying, drive through…

I went in Burger King and asked for a couple of Whoppers. The assistant said I was a handsome devil and that Sheffield Wednesday would win the Premier League…

I was arrested after walking out of Burger King without paying. The police gave me a right old grilling.

The rumour that's going round that I nicked a bottle of vinegar from the chippy; I'm taking the accusations with a pinch of salt.

The wife asked me if I fancied Chinese ship burgers for tea. I said, not more blooming junk food…

I sent our kid out for a Big Mac. Daft lad, he came back with a XXXL raincoat.

*   *   *

I've started work as a waiter. Granted, the money's not fantastic; but at least I can put food on the table…

I went in a greasy-spoon and ordered an all-day breakfast. I started scoffing at 9 o'clock and didn't finish until 5.30.

I told my mate I'd started work at McDonalds. He said, what, flipping burgers, like? I said, flipping burgers? I never realised they got through so many!

Police were called to the greasy spoon after a customer walked out with armfuls of cups, saucers and teaspoons, plus a large quantity of milk and sugar. Eye witnesses said the incident definitely caused a bit of a stir.

Frankenstein, Werewolf and Dracula went out for a meal. Frankenstein and Werewolf ordered a steak. Dracula gulped then went for the black pudding instead...

Waiter: I'm afraid we've overcooked your steak again, sir. Customer: It would be rare if you hadn't.

So I said, waiter, this coffee tastes like mud. He said, what do you expect? It was only ground ten minutes ago.

Speaking of which, I went to a jar of Nescafe's funeral. Talk about coffee mourning.

Did you hear about the policeman who insisted upon eating his T-bone in the pouring rain? He was on a steak out.

I said, waiter, what's this fly doing in my soup? He said, it looks like the breast stroke to me, sir.

*   *   *

Cannibals: they're enough to make your blood boil.

I went to a cannibal's birthday party. We started off with a finger buffet.

1st Cannibal: I wonder why footballers spit so much? 2nd Cannibal: Probably because you leave them on the barbecue too long.

Did you hear about the cannibal that was thrown out of the rock concert after he tried eating the act? He said he'd always been partial to a bit of Meatloaf...

And then there was the cannibal who was dismissed from the army on account of his breakfast habits. Whenever boiled eggs were on the menu, he insisted upon having soldiers with them.

So I said, you really expect me to believe that you've bought a house on a misty island, inhabited by a tribe of cannibals, who hold lengthy debates before deciding who to have for dinner? You're living in cloud-cook-who land...

This starving cannibal said he was going to eat my ticker. I thought, he's a man after my own heart.

I ran for my life when I stumbled across a tribe of rabid cannibals. I thought, they'll have my guts for starters.

Then there was the faddy cannibal who turned his nose up at a portion of poached oil tycoon. He said it was a bit rich for him.

I went to this cannibal's wedding but left in a hurry when I discovered the best man was going to toast me...

What do cannibals have with toast? Baked beings.

*   *   *

I got out of my car and immediately fell over. I was on a slip road.

There were all these people, enjoying a brew at the end of the road. Whey hey, I thought: a tea junction.

Travel News: A large sink-hole has appeared in the fast lane of the M25. The police are looking into it.

I was driving down this road, wondering why everyone was using hand held telephones. Then I realised: I was on the ring road.

So, there I was, standing at the kerb, when this bloke tapped me on the shoulder. He said, do you know there's a zebra crossing back there? I said, is there really? I hope it's having better luck than I am!

Did you hear about the ex-con who was arrested when he got a job painting zigzags around Pelican crossings? Plod said, I thought you were meant to be going straight...?

I was driving down this country lane, dodging in and out of bales of straw. It's the last time you'll catch me on a blooming hay-road, I can tell you.

So I turned the corner there were thousands of angry insects, flying around, stinging pedestrians. Whey hey, I thought: a bee-road.

I was on a carriageway overrun with elephants next. Yup, I was on a trunk road.

As for the bloke who invented bridges: you wouldn't want to cross him.

*   *   *

This sign said: Leeds 46 miles. I thought, that's one heck of a trip for a blooming dog restraint.

Further on, there was another sign, saying: workforce in road, slow. Tell me about it, I thought: six months they've been at it and they're still no nearer finishing.

I stopped and asked this bloke for directions. He said, follow signs for Frogman Edward. After an hour of driving round in circles, I stopped and asked someone else. I said, this chap told me to follow signs for Frogman Edward. He said, sorry, mate, I can't help you; but there's a sign over there for Diver Ted traffic, look...

Off shopping, I passed 23 signs in a row, all saying: Reduce Speed Now. Well, it must have worked; because, when I went in HMV, I spotted the Keanu Reeves film of the same title in the bargain bucket, priced just £1.99.

I was shocked to see three cars in a row, driving over the edge of a cliff after following this big white arrow in the middle of the road. Anyone could see it was a sign, fallen off the side of a Wrigley's gum lorry.

This sign in HMV said: door alarmed. No wonder, I thought; not with Exorcist, the Director's Cut, playing in loop on the next aisle, anyway.

I own a drains unblocking business. The sign on the back of my van says: no stools are left in this vehicle overnight.

This sign outside the restaurant said: kids eat for free. When I got inside, it was full of juvenile goats, munching on grass and weeds.

I spotted a sign saying, Mud on Road. Next thing, I was swerving round this 70s glam rock band, performing hit record, Tiger Feet.

There was this sign in the supermarket, saying, manager's special. I thought, yeah, right; in his dreams, maybe...

I saw a sign saying, ready mix concrete. I thought, I wonder if anyone's thought of telling Mick? He's probably waiting to make a start laying the drive!

* * *

Is Tom Daley a newspaper for alley cats?

Michael Phelps and the Thorpedo: they think they're God's gift to swimming.

So I said, I'm off on a right do tomorrow: a fiver in, drink as much as you want. He said, where's that, like? I said, Barnsley swimming baths.

I applied for this janitor's job at the pool and ended up being made manager instead. Talk about thrown in the deep end.

Patient: Doctor, Doctor, I keep thinking I'm swimming in a big Parisian river. Quack: You're in Seine!

I saw this football referee, jumping in a swimming pool with a bottle of beer. Whey hey, I thought: he's wetting his whistle.

Girl: Dad, Dad, there's a man at the door, collecting for a new swimming pool. Dad: Give him two buckets of water.

This lifeguard stopped me taking a dip in the pool. I said, come on, mate: it's only a small jar of taramasalata…

How many elephants can you get in a swimming pool? A swimming pool full.

What do elephants wear to the swimming baths? Trunks.

*　　*　　*

This sailor told me he'd lost his crow's nest. I said, that's your look out.

As I boarded the cross channel ferry, everybody started jeering at me. It's the last time you'll catch me on a blooming boos cruise, I can tell you…

Bloke goes into the working men's club and slams two U-Boats down on the counter. He says, I've come to pay my subs.

Newsflash: A presenter from hit TV series, I'm a Celebrity Get Me Out of Here, has been mobbed by hordes of ecstatic girl fans, while relaxing on a Caribbean cruise. Witnesses said it was all hands on Dec.

Clambering into the lifeboat, we were stopped in our tracks when the captain appeared from behind an ensemble of clarinets, trumpets and trombones, screaming, no, no, no: I said a band on ship!

A mate of mine delivered a ton fresh herring, a set of hoops and a beach ball to this American warship. Apparently it was for the US Navy Seals.

When the ship sank, I fell madly in love with a girl in the next dingy. It was good while it lasted, like; but we soon drifted apart…

I thought I was seeing things when I spotted a red admiral in the boozer. What the Russian navy were doing out on the lash in Milton Keynes is anyone's guess.

I attended a convention for people who'd escaped desert islands on piles of branches, lashed together with vine. I didn't expect much of a turnout, but it was absolutely packed to the rafters...

I was washed up on this desert island, covered head to toe in red-brown paint. I thought, I can't believe it: I've been marooned...

I entered this competition to see who could last longest without water on a desert island. I won thirst prize.

*   *   *

I hate flying. It doesn't half make my arms ache...

Our kid's new job with British Airways: he reckons he's in it for the long haul.

Well, this time tomorrow I'll be on the plane...I'm taking an inch off the bottom of the door.

I didn't half get a shock when the plane started bouncing down the runway upon take-off. It's the last time you'll get me on a Boing-Boing 737, I can tell you.

I asked my mate how much he paid for his radio controlled German warplane. He said, a hundred nicker off the bloke next door. I said, what a Fokker! He said, tell me about it: the least he could have done was knock me a few quid off!

Bloke goes to the shop and asks for a packet of helicopter crisps. Shopkeeper says, we haven't got helicopter...will plane do?

My iPhone suddenly sprouted wings and began flying circles round the house. It was my own fault for leaving it in airplane mode.

I used to be a pilot in Biblical times. You may have heard of me, in fact: my first name is Pontius.

I went to this fancy dress party and got talking to a policeman in a Messerschmitt 109 costume. I said, are you in plane-clothes...?

Did you hear about the Scottish Kamikaze pilot that crashed his plane into his brother's scrap yard?

Today's conundrum: why did Kamikaze pilots wear helmets...?

*   *   *

ET's been caught shoplifting. I always said he was light fingered.

I went in Curry's and asked about Blu-ray. They put a call out and this bloke appeared. It said Raymond on his shirt and he was completely blue from head to foot.

So, there I was, getting stuck into the weekly shop, when this bloke emptied a packet of grated cheese over my head. I said, that was mature, wasn't it...?

Humming a tune round HMV, I said, is that The Carpenters I can hear? Assistant said, no, but there's a plumber out back, unblocking the loo...

So I said, where will I find The Pet Shop Boys? Assistant turned to his mate and said, I think the nearest one's on the other side of town, isn't it...?

A cashier in this Swedish, self-assembly furniture shop remarked how tired I looked after an 18 mile walk to the store. I said, tell me about: I wish you'd take that flipping sign down, insisting people hike here...

Upon hearing the Incredible Hulk was opening a fruit and veg shop on the high street, one angry local resident was heard to say, it's a chippy we need: not another blooming green grocer!

I asked the wife to nip down the shops for corned beef, potatoes, leeks, carrots and onions. I said, and try not to make a hash of it...

I took my iPhone back to the shop when it started leaking water. I said, I think it might have been tapped.

Window shopping with the wife, I pointed out this diamond encrusted Rolex. I said, that's the one I'd get. Next thing, Cyclops had me pinned against a wall. He said, you wanna piece of me…?

I sent our kid out for a ball of wool. Five minutes later, his mate turned up, wanting to know where he was. I said, he's gone…but not for cotton.

My new job at the supermarket: I can't Co-op.

*   *   *

I'm taking over at the bakery. It's a bun deal…

The wife asked if I'd remembered to fetch the bread. I said, sorry, darling; it never crust my mind…

Why did the extinct bird apply for a job at the bakery? Because it kneaded the dough-dough.

The bakery football team's star midfielder was sitting cross-legged in the centre circle, munching on a tuna and mayonnaise baguette. Apparently the gaffer had given him a free roll.

I stopped off at the bakers, then called in the spiritualist church on the way home. This bloke said, what are you, a medium, like? Wiping fresh cream from my mouth, I said, certainly am, mate. Not for much longer, though; not with the way these buns are going down, anyway…

Bloke goes in the bakery and asks for a wasp. Assistant says, we don't sell wasps, sir. Bloke says, yes, you do: there's one in the window, look.

27 years after starting work at the bread shop, the wife's suddenly decided she hates it. The boss reckons she's going through a mid-loaf crisis.

A bloke with bright red hair has bought the bakers shop. He's a ginger bread man.

That nice girl at the bakery: by all accounts she's got a bun in the oven.

Why did the sausage roll? Because it saw the apple turn over.

*   *   *

I didn't get that job at the snooker club. Rumour has it I wasn't even in the frame.

I turned up at the pub in my swimming trunks. Alright, I said, where's this blooming pool table?

It's just been on the radio that a lorry load of snooker extensions has overturned, blocking the motorway. Drivers have been told to expect long cues...

Bloke goes to the quacks, feeling unwell after surviving six months on a diet of snooker balls. Quack says, any particular colours, like? He said, reds and yellows mainly and the occasional blue, black and brown. Quack says, you know your problem, don't you? You're not getting enough greens!

My idea of booking a table for the girlfriend's birthday was a complete disaster. She didn't pot a single ball.

There was this girl in the pub, balancing a pint of lager on her head, while playing snooker and reciting snippets from Peter the Rabbit. Whey hey, I thought: beer-tricks-potter...

When our kid got this tip off, he got straight on the phone to the police. I don't think they were best pleased when they turned up and were presented with a dodgy snooker cue.

I stopped off for a pint at Potters Bar. Never again, I can tell you: it was full of drunken snooker players.

What's green, got six legs and could hurt you if it fell out of a tree? A snooker table.

I said, doctor, doctor, I keep thinking I'm a snooker ball. He said, you and everyone else today, matey; now get to the back of the cue.

Did you hear about the drug dealing snooker player that went pot...?

*   *   *

Golfing shoes for sale. Hole in one.

This sign said, don't phone while driving. I thought, surely no one's daft enough to practise their golf swing in the fast lane...?

It's just been on the news that Irish golfer, Rory McIlroy, has won a Major. Apparently he's 72-years old, graduated from Sandhurst, and was decorated for gallantry in the Balkans.

What would you get if you crossed a boy magician with Tiger Woods? Harry Putter.

I was on the 18th hole when this German car went flying over my head and demolished the clubhouse. Apparently it was someone having a game of Volkswagen Golf.

So, there I was, drowning in quicksand, when my mobile rang. It was my bezzie mate, asking if I fancied a quick nine holes. I said, I'd love to, pal; but unfortunately I'm up to my neck in it at the moment...

We threw ourselves to the ground when the shout went up: Fore! I said to my mate: Stay down: there's three more to come yet!

After winning £133m on Euro Millions, I treated myself to a set of golf clubs: Sunningdale, St Andrews and Muirfield.

I went to this golf tournament where all the players were wearing cloaks and mortar boards. It was the Masters.

I always have breakfast on the golf course: tee 'n' toast.

*   *   *

Tennis: what a racket.

Andy Murray's car for sale. 6 month's tax, MOT and full service history.

I've just been sacked from my job at the tennis ball factory. No worries, though; I'll soon bounce back...

A vicious serve hit the champion right where it hurt. The umpire said, new balls, please...

Patient: Doctor, doctor, I keep thinking I'm John McEnroe. Quack: You *cannot* be serious!

I'm having trouble getting on the Lawn Tennis Association website. I think they might be having trouble with the server.

When the umpire called the ball out, the ball accepted and they had a fight round the back of the changing rooms.

Did you hear about the gay tennis player that won in straight sets?

Two vicars playing tennis. Umpire says, first service, please...

What time does Roger Federer go to bed? Tennish.

*   *   *

I finished up getting Sky in the end. My roof blew off.

I put a call into BT Vision. They said to try Specsavers.

Speaking of which, guess who I bumped into in the opticians? Everybody I saw!

TV guides: I'm sick of them leading expeditions round the back of the telly.

I refused to allow a dodgy brightness issue to spoil my enjoyment of Return of the Jedi. That said, I must admit it was a bit on the dark side.

So I said, I got absolutely hammered last night, watching classic sitcoms on TV. She said, Last of the Summer Wine, like? I said, try a bottle of gin and a case of strong lager…

I went on The Apprentice and Lord Sugar sent me to the stores for a left-handed screwdriver and a long stand. I came back three hours later with a tin of Tartan paint.

I had a TV dinner last night: the flat screen was lovely toasted, but some of the components were a bit on the tough side.

What a load of rubbish This is Your Life is. I didn't get mentioned once.

I auditioned for the X-Factor and got packed straight off to boot camp. Oh my God, I thought: I've just joined the marines…

That bloke on Thunderbirds asks a lot of questions, doesn't he? He's a right nosey Parker.

I've just been watching Steven Hawking's Universe. It was a really good programme, like; but I didn't know he owned it…

This woman rattled a jar under my nose and asked if I'd like to donate to charity. I said, would I heckers like: those Emmerdale Dingles earn twenty times what I do.

Him: I reckon a Singer will win Britain's Got Talent. Her: Don't talk daft: there's not even a sewing machine in it.

Choreographers? Are they experts on Coronation Street?

*   *   *

I stayed up till midnight, watching this documentary about mods. Honestly, I must have been off my rocker.

Straight after, it was a programme about shipbuilding on the Clyde. Riveting.

Followed by a documentary on North Sea oil exploration. *Bo-ring.*

Then a programme detailing how one in fifty people in the UK are borderline alcoholic. Staggering.

Oh, and another depicting an alarming increase in the use of police tasers? Stunning.

I have to say the documentary about Dalmatian dogs was spot on, mind.

And how can I forget that brilliant programme, depicting the torture endured by OCD sufferers? It was so good, in fact, I watched it 183 times.

Not like the documentary about life in an underwear factory. What a load of pants that was.

As for that programme, illustrating how winged insects use suction to adhere themselves to vertical surfaces...I have to say it's the best fly on the wall documentary I've ever seen!

Speaking of flies, I swatted three of the blighters earlier: two males and a female. How did I know which was which? Because the males were on beer cans and the female was on the phone.

If a fly didn't have wings, would it be a walk...?

*   *   *

I watched The Exorcist and it scared me half to death. Now I'm worried what will happen if I put it on again.

I'll not be in a hurry to watch Zulu again, I can tell you. It was about a toilet attendant at Chester Zoo!

I didn't reckon much to that A-Team movie, either. If you ask me, it was all about Face.

Our kid turned down a role in a film about a family of mouse-like creatures, living on a distant moon, speaking in whistles, while eating soup from the Soup Dragon. Personally, I think he dropped a right Clanger...

That film's on again later, the one where occupants of an Antarctic research station discover an alien in a block of ice then battle to stay alive as it consumes them one by one. Straight after, it's the remake. Honestly, if it's not one Thing it's another...

The film, 127 Hours, where a bloke gets trapped in a canyon then cuts his own arm off to escape: it was a brilliant storyline, like; but I really think it should be renamed 94 minutes.

So, there I was, watching this Bruce Lee classic, when the missus arrived home early to spoil the ending. Talk about Enter the Dragon.

This bloke asked me if I was well up on the chronological order of movies starring Keanu Reeves. I said, I'd reckon I'm pretty much up to Speed...

Edward Scissorhands put in a scintillating performance for the Hollywood football team. The gaffer said he'd never seen him looking so sharp.

I forgot to record science fiction thriller, Knowing, starring Nicholas Cage. Not to worry. I mean, it's not like it's the end of the world, is it?

Gingers Rogers and Fred Astaire: they were alright, like; but I wouldn't make a song and dance about them.

I got this job on security at the Oscars. Four o'clock in the morning, this posh looking actress turned up, arm in arm with Hugh Grant. Whey hey, I thought: it's Elizabeth Early...

I bumped into Steven Spielberg, lost on his way to the Oscars. I said, you know your trouble, don't you, mate? You've no sense of direction.

So I said, where's Panavision, Mr Spielberg? He said, never heard of it. I said, liar, liar, pants on fire: your last movie was filmed there.

Vin Diesel, Stallone and Schwarzenegger were in a casting session for a new film about classical European composers. Schwarzenegger said, I'll be Bach...

*   *   *

It's just been on the news that the local sewage works is facing closure. Apparently two million jobbies are at risk.

Why do farts smell? For the benefit of deaf people, of course.

I've just bought a new toilet. Nothing fancy, just bog standard.

Mr & Mrs Bagshaw, their two sons, four daughters, grandma and grandad, aunts, uncles, cousins and half-cousins, all came down with diahorrea on the same day. Runs in the family by the sounds of it.

I'm next in line for the throne. In actual fact, I'd be on it already if trap 2 hadn't been out of order.

Fitting a motion detector in the bathroom wasn't the best idea I've ever had. Every time someone does a jobbie, the blooming alarm goes off!

The wife lost the diamond out of her ring during dinner. Now she sticks her head down the pot every time she goes to the loo, convinced it will turn up eventually. Talk about going through the motions...

I went to the chemist and that woman was in again, the one who used to work at McDonalds. I said, a box of laxatives, please. She said, to go? I said, what do you think…?

I withdrew my offer on this house when the estate agent said there was no chain. I said, what's the point if I can't flush the blooming loo…?

Don't forget it's the AGM of the weak bladder association tonight. If you can't make it, just give us a tinkle.

It was a disappointing night at the Constipation Society AGM. Not a single motion was passed.

A pal of mine got his head stuck in the pot. I don't think I've ever seen him so down in the dumps.

Someone let a hand grenade off in the high street toilets: bang out of order!

I found a toilet in a field. Talk about pot luck.

*   *   *

Quack: It's my sad duty to inform you that you've contracted a virulent flesh eating bug. World's fattest man: How long have I got? Quack: About fifty years...

This fitness instructor suggested I try aerobics. I said, can you please explain how eating chocolate covered biros is going to help me lose weight...?

I'm on a crash diet. I keep driving my car into brick walls, meaning I spend all my wages on repairs and have nothing left for food.

I'm not saying my girlfriend's got a sweet tooth; but when I asked her which person in the world she most admired, she said, it's got to be Mr Kipling...

So I said, I can't believe how much weight I've put on. Perhaps I've got an over active, erm, erm...She said, thyroid gland? I said, no, knife and fork!

I wouldn't say our kid's overweight; but he's just been stopped on his way out of the bowling alley and accused of having a ball up his top.

I went to see a dietician after gaining 3-stones in two weeks since starting my new job. She said, what do you do? I said, I'm a product-tester in a pork pie factory...

The crowd roared with applause as I took my turn in the cheeseburger charity challenge. Talk about clapping weight on.

I'm not saying I'm unfit, like; but two minutes into my debut as a referee's assistant, I was already starting to flag...

I didn't reckon much to that yo-yo dieting lark. Every time I swallowed one, it came straight back up again.

*   *   *

I'll swear I'm turning into a shark: I'm going fin on top.

This bloke asked me if I knew where he could get a new wig from. I said, not off the top of my head.

I grew my hair over my eyes then signed on for the local football club. Not that I ever made the team: I was just a fringe player...

Apparently Rovers have signed this big, pink footballer, covered in yellow spots, with long strands of hair combed meticulously across his scalp. Rumours are it's Blobby Charlton.

I went to the barbers for a number 2. I don't think old misery guts was best pleased when I dropped my pants and started squatting in the corner...

The woman next door booked an appointment with a mobile hairdresser. You should have seen the look on her face when this iPhone 7 turned up with curling tongs and a pair of scissors.

I scored with a curler on my debut for the Dog & Duck footie team. It was still in my hair from the night before and the ball skimmed it on the way in.

The M6 was closed today after a lorry load of toupees collided with lorry load of Chewbacca onesies. Witnesses described the incident as hairy.

Barber: Crew cut, sir? Sailor: I'm afraid not: the rest of the lads are already at sea, steaming for Gibraltar.

I wasn't sure about my new hair transplant at first. But I have to admit it's growing on me...

*   *   *

Chiropodists: they don't half earn their corn...

I used to go out with a chiropodist, in fact. She was a real fun gal.

I went for a trainee cobbler's job. This bloke said, so, have you ever soled shoes before? I said, you bet; I used to be senior sales assistant at Timpson's...

First shift at the shoe shop, this bloke holding a slip-on asked the wife if he could try it on. The good news is that his swelling is going down now and there's a small chance he'll be out of hospital before the weekend.

I was shocked to discover I'd been given a severed head for my birthday. The next parcel I opened contained a torso, and the one after that an arm and then a leg. With several more still to go, I thought: hmm; something's definitely afoot...

So I said, did you see Brogue Traders last night? He said, don't you mean Rogue Traders? I said, no, Brogue: it was all about a job lot of dodgy shoes.

Him: What leather makes the best shoes? Her: No idea...but banana skins definitely make the best slippers!

They've stopped selling Lucozade in Boots: it comes out of the lace holes.

I attended a shoe repairer's convention. It was a right load of cobblers.

She said, I've got a hole in my sock. I said, darn it...

*   *   *

I'm putting money away for a rainy day. I'm saving up for a new brolly.

So I said, it's raining cats and dogs out there, sweetheart. She said, be careful you don't tread in any poodles, darling…

The weatherman said it might be cold; but, on the other hand, it could be sunny. So, just to be safe, I left home with one glove on and one glove off.

I was reading this funny text message when I looked out of the window and saw there was a hurricane heading my way. Talk about LOL before the storm.

The weatherman has warned to expect plenty of wind on Tuesday. Apparently it's national mushy peas day.

When the forecast said to prepare for a touch of frost, the last thing I expected to find was David Jason, camped out on the front lawn…

A local weatherman has been blamed for the decision to rename Manchester, Santiago; this after predicting the region would be turning a bit Chile.

Bloke goes in the DVD shop. He says, can you recommend a decent Disney film? Assistant says, you like a Frozen man to me. Bloke says, I'm not surprised. It's blowing a blooming blizzard outside.

Walking down the street, I was surrounded by dozens of people, dressed as world famous Yorkshire talk show hosts. When I arrived home, the wife asked if it was nice out. I said, not bad…a bit Parky, like.

During the recent spell of severe weather, the government advised people to wear hi-vis clothing and carry the following items at all times:

blanket, shovel, flask, spare batteries, a jerry-can of petrol, and 72-hours-worth of food and water. Honestly, I felt such an idiot, climbing aboard the number 22 bus this morning.

I've just resigned from my gritter-driver's job at Humberside county council. They've asked me to reconsider, but I've told them no chance: Hull can freeze over first.

I nearly got run over by a snow plough. Watch where you're going, I shouted...through gritted teeth.

Our kid's announced his engagement just 24-hours after falling in love in the middle of a tornado. Talk about whirlwind romance.

What did the female tornado say to the female hurricane? A gale's got to do what a gale's got to do.

The long range weather forecast says no rain for six months. Somehow, though, I drought it...

*　　*　　*

Printed in Great Britain
by Amazon